INTOXIDATED

What love is, how to find it, and how not to

based on a decade of my disastrous dating decisions.

(The sex education you won't get in school.)

♥

by Laura Elizabeth

ISBN 978-1-09835-263-9

TABLE OF CONTENTS

6

PART III – LOVE LIMBO

"Healing is a matter of time,
but it is sometimes also a matter of opportunity."
Hippocrates

Special thanks to

my sister and closest friends

for being there even when you didn't have to.

I love you.

♥

Mom & Dad,

Thank you for supporting me through my unique case of curiosity.

I love you.

♥

14

To all the men I was
"romantically"
involved with prior to writing this,
(including those not mentioned)

Thank you for sharing a part of your life and yourself with me.

♥

WHO AM I?

"Honesty and transparency make you vulnerable.
Be honest and transparent anyway."
Mother Teresa

My obsession with boys started before I even realized it; I had crushes on boys as early as preschool. I used to chase them on the playground until the bell rang, but seemed I was never able to catch the ones I liked. What could possibly be engrained in a young girl's head that would condition her to physically *run* after boys at that age?

In middle and high school, I fell for the *relationship concept* instead of falling for the boy. Do you know what happens when you fall for something that doesn't catch you?

You crash.

This mindset followed me through my twenties before the universe finally put a stop to it. A resulting heartbreak is the crash and burn of emotion best remedied by ice cream, our closest friends, buckets of tears and in most cases, complete removal of the individual that is a source of that pain from our life. The wreckage is then either let go of or stored away in a compartment of our brains only to be brought out by the next person that coincidentally does something that triggers us of that traumatic time from the past...

***

My generation, "the millennials," exists in a dating world the human race has never experienced before—a virtual one. Millions of potential bachelors and bachelorettes are available at our fingertips; yet somehow we are growing more disconnected than any generation before us. How could we have so much opportunity, yet be headed in the opposite direction of finding what we actually want? Has the integration of technology in our dating lives doomed us all in the arena of love forever? Are millennials so spoiled and lazy that we don't know what it's like to work for what we want? Let's define a few things so we can start on the same page.

For starters—What is "dating?"

A *date*, according to Merriam-Webster's Dictionary, is defined as a "*romantic* social arrangement." Seems pretty straight forward, but one word can be broken down a bit further—

What, exactly, is "*romantic*?"

The dictionary has some very interesting input here, which I think is why there's so much confusion as to what constitutes as a "date" in the first place. *Romance* is a noun described by emotion, love, and *lack of basis in all things factual*. Therefore by definition, romance and dating are literally both fairytale-esque things. "They" say romanticism is dead... so does that mean that only the dead seek romanticism? Why do we waste our youth trying to locate our "soulmate?" We are led to believe this "soulmate" will complete us. Why do we believe we are not whole in the first place?

Regardless of how you interpret the word "soulmate," how are we supposed to find that person? With traditional methods of dating nearing extinction, is embarking on "dates" with strangers from the internet all it's cracked up to be? Does it even work? Talking to strangers is a great way for us to get out of our comfort zone, which also happens to be when we grow and learn the most about ourselves. For years I was trying to find the right person in all the wrong ways and I hope that by sharing the stories that follow I can help other lonely people understand how to navigate the world of love and dating. Making mistakes is the most effective way to learn anything but *hearing stories* about them is more efficient.

Generally, we decide within the first few minutes of meeting someone if we are attracted to them, and when we are, it is merely human nature to want to get closer; though we must be aware of the intentions behind our interactions. If we want someone enough, we start trying too hard to be someone we are not—*the person we <u>think</u> they want.*

We can be so nervous about being ourselves that we aren't! At no rate will we connect with anyone we're attracted to if this is how our interactions go. How does an initial attraction result in a loving relationship? Is there a formula or equation for finding love?

What if we all really just want the same thing?

It is when we *expect* reciprocation that we are disappointed.

Even if we don't get along with our parents or siblings or significant other all the time, most of us still choose to love them because love is bigger than that. We are led to believe through movies and television and stories that love should be romantic (remember, by definition this is an imaginary concept) and we'll have a "happily ever after" once we "fall in love" with our "soulmate." And maybe we do, I'm not sure. I'm still before the after, whatever that means.

Here's another fun one—What does it mean to *"fall in love,"* and why would anyone even want to? Falling in general usually hurts. I certainly collected my fair share of scrapes and bruises throughout the years due to my behavior. The men who tripped me up taught me critical life lessons of human tendencies, the way we love and connect with each other, and plenty of other stuff completely unrelated to the topics of this book (such as how to shotgun a beer or throw a football).

Emotions make it difficult for us to understand and see "love" clearly when we are young. We use the word "love" in a couple different ways. Those who do not understand the concept often use them interchangeably. Love is easy to explain but I'm not going to outline it for you in the introduction.

First, I have to un-brainwash you.

We devalue the word "love" by using it for *things*—

Pizza. Chocolate. Wine. Coffee. Shopping. Travel...

We don't actually love this stuff, we just like them a lot; maybe <u>too</u> much in some circumstances. We enjoy them because they make us feel good. The utter pleasure these things bring to us creates a unique emotional experience where gratification (a feeling of pleasure or satisfaction) that we equate to happiness (a state of being). This nostalgic, positive feeling we remember is why we continuously find ourselves consuming these things.

Imagine how much that nostalgic feeling comes into play during the dating process...

When a person hugs or kisses us, we then have a *physical* feeling to associate with them (in addition to the emotional one) which may be good, bad or even something in between. When we see them again or even think about them, that feeling may resurface to our consciousness and until we understand why we feel it and until we know what it means, we will misinterpret our own feelings.

In today's society we are led to believe *everybody* loves sex—and I won't lie to you, it can be pretty freaking amazing. Most people want it for the pleasure and connection, some of us even believe we *need* it, yet, few are getting it regularly, if at all. Once you understand it, it is extraordinarily easy to get (...though it may or may not be through means that are ethical and moral).

Many have tried to figure out what the perfect amount of sex is by observing others and collecting data on them instead of getting out there and figuring it out for themselves. We've all seen the statistics in books and articles, but they are trying to measure something that is simply immeasurable. Such results prove nothing other than what is currently "normal," which is clearly not serving us as a species. Is following the crowd the best option? The primary reason we settle for normalcy is to avoid the judgement for being different. When we believe we are normal, we believe we fit in. How unfortunate is it that "normal" is what so many of us strive for?

Both sex itself or the absence of it can very easily destroy any relationship. Knowing this, how is it possible for there to be a universal "perfect amount?"

***

What is now this book started off as my personal journal. I am not good at talking about my feelings; I avoid them at all costs (chances are, you can relate). Reflecting on my past in this way forced me to overcome my fear of talking about my feelings by first acknowledging them to myself. No one wants to have a conversation about something they don't understand, and I believe the primary reason people don't talk about feelings is because we don't fully understand our own. It's much easier to sweep them under the rug and numb ourselves with other feelings (often induced by drugs). The problem then becomes that it's going to be a mess under that dusty rug once you're finally sober enough to clean what's there.

Several people in my life suggested that I start a journal as a means of therapy and years went by before I actually listened to one of them. When I finally did, it progressed into the unloading of an entire decade of emotional baggage. To get all the stuff out of my head and into the form of written word helped me since I was too stubborn to seek outside help. Journaling enabled me to observe my problems from an entirely new perspective and provided me with the opportunity to evaluate my own thoughts for incongruencies so that I may address them accordingly.

The stories that follow are about completely made-up characters based on my interactions with wonderful people, and the perceived relations that transpired between us are *the sum of both our choices*. This is some type of an interpretation of those memories. You and I both know there are two sides to every story.

While I always enjoyed writing, I never once considered being an author because I was taught to focus on my mathematics, science, business and computer skills since those were the things required to make money in today's society (according to my parents… and after years of walking in that direction, I can confirm this holds true). My main objective is to help you understand what love is and how anyone can find it by sharing my countless failures that equate to be a disastrously wild and beautifully painful love life. Hopefully sharing these stories can make a positive impact on our collective dating culture and mental health.

Before you judge, these are not "letters to lost lovers" or some other sappy love story nonsense. This is the REAL story.

***

I'm extremely curious by nature. Love, sex, dating and relationships have always fascinated me but in order to figure out what any of those things even were, I had to see and experience them for myself. As a child, I was sheltered from all things sexual and was never allowed to date or consume any romance-related media, including television, music and movies. My mother attempted to raise a proper lady and my options as a child were to be what was expected of me or punished unless I agreed to conform. I was always in trouble for something. When I had questions about the topic of social norms or sex, instead of an explanation, I received a "because I said so," "because that's how a lady acts," or "because that's what the Bible says."

Such responses do not constitute as "answers" in my book. When I was old enough, I read the kid's version of the Bible in hopes that it would provide some answers, but because there was never any tangible proof to back it up, I considered even that to be a fairytale, forever categorized in my mind with Disney movies and ancient myths. One boy and one girl animal of a bunch of different species on the same boat? *Come on.* Even as a kid I wasn't convinced—and I actually believed in Santa Claus at one point in my childhood.

Curiosity is only alleviated by exploration. Exploration yields information, which then leads to further curiosity, and consequently the cycle repeats itself. Learning is the only commitment that will bring us eternal happiness because there is no limit to the amount of information we may seek and absorb.

***

At the time that I wrote this, I was reaching the end of my roaring twenties. Like the rest of corporate America, I worked a standard nine-to-five job as a bookkeeper and spent many of those hours daydreaming about being someplace else, as most of us do. With that said, I am incredibly grateful for my employment at that establishment and I sincerely respect the people running it.

My upbringing is one of the classic American Dream household. I have one brother and one sister, Dad worked, Mom took care of us. I was raised in small-ish town in a cookie-cutter neighborhood with a bunch of other kids my age, most of which were boys. Those were the people I spent the majority of my daylight hours during my teenage years.

I never felt like I had anyone I could talk to about emotions, boys or dating, so I resorted to learning through the experimental procedure of trial and error; which as we all know, consists primarily of errors—just ask the ghosts of Albert Einstein or Thomas Edison. There are so many smart, attractive and funny single people out there waiting to connect with the right person. I met a ton of them;

they just weren't my "Prince Charming." Complaining that there is a lack of desirable and eligible single people out there is the first problem of many single people. The secret to connection is mindset. You'll never connect with anyone if you don't believe you will.

Now that you know a little about me and where I came from, let's get started. Time to go on an adventure filled with all kinds of stuff: *Crying. Laughing. Love. Friendship. Anger. Loneliness. Regret. Passion. Control. Emotional abuse. Ethics. Rape. Drugs. Cheating. Morals. Virginity. Freedom. Friends with benefits. Depression. Rock bottom... And so much more.*

To fully understand anything, we must know what it is like to be both with and without that thing. This is challenging to accomplish because it requires the ability to achieve two different perspectives. That's what I'm going to use this rest of this book to demonstrate.

When I first entered the dating world, I was incredibly naïve. It's women like me who make the dating scene complicated in the first place. Here are twenty-six things I wish I learned *before* I entered the world looking for love where I instead found twenty-six teachers (which isn't all that bad to be honest). People have been asking me for years why I'm single, and my answer is usually something to the effect of "I haven't found the right person." I think we all tell ourselves that, but the truth is we have not yet found ourselves. Why do we waste so much of our lives searching for a soulmate in someone else before figuring out who we really are?

My hope is that by adding this information to the universal collective we can better understand how relationships develop between men and women and spread awareness to heal the toxic behaviors and patterns we are taught about dating in modern

Western culture. Knowledge is power and asking the right questions is the key to unlocking it. What if life is more like Jeopardy than we ever considered?

*

CAUTIONARY DISCLAIMER

*"I am always doing that which I cannot do,
in order that I may learn how to do it."*
Vincent Van Gogh

The title of this book alone may lead you to believe I have been involved with a lot of people, and I will argue that it depends on the number of people YOU have been with by comparison— What's your bias? Everything in life is a matter of perspective, and as Theodore Roosevelt once said, "Comparison is the thief of joy."

Over the course of a decade, I probably met somewhere in the ballpark of fifty men from the internet in person and exchanged contact information with close to a hundred men I met in bars. I probably also exchanged digits with another hundred men who initiated conversations with me at gas stations, coffee shops, laundromats, grocery stores, airports, or other everyday locations people frequent. I attribute this to my physical appearance, positive attitude and the frequency of which I am out in the world instead of sitting on my couch watching TV, for example.

I saw the good, the bad, the ugly and the abhorrent; a lot of it being my own behavior. I'm unquestionably no angel; I did many things I am not proud of; and don't worry, I'll share those, too. None of us are perfect. The words in this book explain how situations unfolded from my perspective and my analysis of those interactions from a future version of myself. Alcohol is also a recurring character in these stories. I am still making mistakes to this day and will always accept that I have a lot left to learn. Through the decade of my life experiences that I share with you in the pages that follow, my beliefs change and evolve as they are repeatedly influenced by the results of my own curiosity and the people I chose to surround myself with.

There are going to be a few things in this book that may be uncomfortable to read. Had I handled them differently, I may have potentially blocked them from happening; but there's no use in entertaining alternate scenarios. It is far more constructive to work on developing the skills necessary to prevent history from repeating itself. I must accept responsibility for getting myself into those nightmare predicaments to begin with.

With *that* out of the way, I don't want you to think that your love, dating, or sex life will magically improve or change after reading this book. That is completely dependent on what you want to take away from this. Things don't change unless you *want* change; and if you can't change something, you might have to change your mind. I was never someone who listened to other people's empty advice; I want to understand <u>WHY</u>. Someone may tell me over and over to do something but unless I am able to comprehend *how* they came to that conclusion, I will likely still choose to make the mistake; I habitually learn things the hard way. Maybe if a book like this existed prior to my entering into the dating world, I wouldn't get myself into so much mischief... but then again, I probably still would. It's just who I am.

*

Part I
Serial Monogamy

ONE

ADRIAN

*"A library is a place where you can lose your
innocence without losing your virginity."*
Germaine Greer

Today was not an ordinary day.

For the first time in my life, I was minutes away from going
on a first date with a boy. I anxiously stared out my parents' window
at the street awaiting his arrival. He was already eighteen and had
his own car so he was picking me up. We only met a few times but
since we knew tons of the same people, it was safe to trust him
(though strangers from the internet taking us from one place to
another is the new normal, I digress).

The date was one of traditional sorts—lunch and a movie,
and we shared our first kiss somewhere in between. I wondered if
he thought I was a good at it, but what does that even mean? How
does someone become a good kisser? It would be a while before I
figured out, but I thought that if I was a good kisser, he would like
me more (a result of people-pleasing behavior I picked up in
childhood). Many people throughout my twenties told me I should
stop letting people walk all over me but I never understood how it
was actually affecting my life. I get it now. People-pleasers absorb
the toxicity of others until they themselves begin to exude the same
toxic behaviors.

Our faces were practically glued together that day. We kissed a lot. After the movie let out, we strolled around the nearby shopping areas to prolong our time together before he had to give me back to my parents. Sure enough, we almost immediately ran into someone he knew and they exchanged friendly "hello's" before Adrian abruptly looked back at me—

"Oh! This is my girlfriend, Laura."

Though I was caught off guard, this was thrilling news for me. *Was this it?* Was he the real deal? Were we going to get married and have babies and grow old together? We would see our families on Sundays and attend our kids' sports games on Saturdays and… I lost my footing. Down the rabbit hole I fell.

He didn't *ask* me to be his girlfriend—he just introduced me that way. I had an idea engrained in my mind about how it would happen and he completely skipped that step. I thought it would be a magical moment like a proposal, that he would say, "Laura, will you be my girlfriend?" and I would say "YES!" and then we would live happily ever after. Ha!

We later had a conversation about it so we were able to clear the air on the subject. It irritated me because he assumed how I felt; however, I can pretend like it bothered me all day but at the end of it, I was too fixated on the idea of having a boyfriend to care all that much. Finally, after years of being jealous of everyone else for having someone to hug and kiss, I could finally be in love with someone, too. My parents never allowed me to date anyone before Adrian, though I had my fair share of "boyfriends" before him as well; though with the absence of any physical affection.

Having a boyfriend was a big deal. For the first time since I learned how to lose a virginity, I had someone to lose my virginity to. Sex, as they say, is like a drug. Once you get it once, you want it again both because of the physical sensation resulting from the chemical changes in our bodies as well as the intense emotional connection that may be experienced when you truly want to be with someone. As a young adult, it is nearly impossible to comprehend this because we are too inexperienced to distinguish between the two and gullible enough to believe the narrative pushed by society, which suggests that sex itself is absolutely amazing and everyone is and should be basically doing it all the time for fun.

Exhibit A: Me. (Well, for a decade, anyway. Not currently.)

Sex was this mysterious thing everyone seemed to know more about than I did. It is ordinary for any teenager to be interested in sex, but I was a unique case. I thought I *needed* to do it to have a boyfriend. All the cool kids were talking about it and in almost every movie I wasn't permitted to see by my parents, some combination of characters have sex, do other stuff, or at least have a conversation about it. I was always missing the punchline of jokes with my friends because I had no clue what anything was. Sex was everywhere I looked and listened, but I was never able to see or hear it. Upon my release into the wild, I knew literally nothing about sex aside from how it works, plain and simple...

Penis → Vagina

Sex is a puzzle that requires only two pieces for completion, and by default I have one. That's all you need to know, right? It's not rocket science; it's the most natural thing our bodies can do.

Back in middle school when my classmates were apparently learning how to put a condom on a banana, I was extracted from the room and redirected to the library to read miscellaneous articles and write essays about animals or history or some other random stuff. It truly felt like a punishment. Sexual education was an exclusive club and I was the only one who didn't get initiated because my mother refused to sign the form enabling me to participate. She believed it to be inappropriate for children to be learning about the sexual functions of the human body because the narrative pushed by the public school system is not one of abstinence (as the case is with religion). Though I do not believe children should be sexually active, I do believe sheltering a person from anything makes that thing a point of greater interest to them.

Bless my parents' souls for trying to keep me healthy, happy and out of trouble despite my particularly curious nature. No parent knows what they're doing and for just a second, imagine being mine! They had no idea what they were getting themselves into.

My only "sexual education" consisted of them sitting me down at the dinner table one afternoon, spreading an anatomy book out on the table, pointing at the penis and vagina, and explaining how a baby is formed. It was so awkward, I wanted nothing more than to get the heck out of there. There was nothing about protection. There was nothing about feelings. There was nothing about pleasure. I was told not to have sex unless I was married and ready to make babies because that's what sex is for. Period.

No exceptions.

Naturally, I thought everything my parents were telling me about the topic was complete garbage. Why would all the other kids in my class be spending days learning about sex but this was the only conversation I was getting, and it was only a few minutes long?

There had to be more. I refused to believe it.

Because I did not know much else, all I knew for sure was that I wanted to do it. I didn't care who or what or when or where. I just knew I wanted to find my future husband pronto so I could give my V-card to him and start living my best life already. I waited for Adrian long enough.

As you might imagine, Adrian was genuinely elated to show me what this sex thing was all about. Not on that first date, anyway, but another day—watching the sunset in the backseat of a car after eating spectacularly tasty cheeseburgers. It was exactly what I wanted and it was exactly as I expected... a penis entering a vagina.

My first intercourse experience was neither disappointing nor satisfying; but rather, left me somewhat perplexed... *This* is what people are so obsessed with? What's the big deal? I anticipated sex was going to feel magical since that's what everyone claimed. Maybe I was doing something wrong? Adrian had sex before and because I was a newb, I assumed he knew what he was doing. Clearly I was missing something in addition to climaxing, or perhaps the problem was simply that I lacked experience with myself. Regardless, he had his happy ending, which was a relief for me—at least something went right.

Though it was certainly one of the more bizarre nights of my life, my feelings for Adrian were stronger than ever. We were both "weird," for lack of a better word, and we were never really in alignment with the opinions set forth by modern society, in two drastically different ways. When I was with him, I felt like I finally had someone who understood me because no one understood him either or why I was with him. Around him, I felt that innocent, dreamy Justin Bieber variety of love; one where he called me "baby" and simply gazing into his sparkling eyes made all my worries melt away.

***

A number of intimate experiences later, the condom broke.

It is in testing moments like these that we begin asking ourselves new questions and looking at things from alternative perspectives. As much as I wanted to have a future with Adrian, we were not interested in becoming stars on the next season of MTV's *Teen Mom* so we resorted to Plan B. (In case you don't know, that's a morning-after pill.)

Pregnancy would by far be the worst way for my parents to learn that I was sexually active, or so I thought at the time... this book may arguably be worse. Back then they would probably take me for a chastity belt fitting had they known. There's no doubt in my mind that Adrian will be a great father one day, but the idea of having a dependent, baby human with a dependent, adult Adrian terrified the hell out of me. Thankfully, nothing came of it other than Adrian himself.

***

Months passed. I was ignoring all the people in my life who mattered because my craving to be in round-the-clock contact with Adrian was the only thing I could focus on. I was drunk in love and too busy riding out the high to pay attention to any of them, and in turn they grew to dislike Adrian.

The hangover was slowly creeping in. Our relationship consisted mostly of sex, time with *his* family and friends, watching shows or movies, and talking to, arguing, and listening to each other breathe over the phone. Phone calls once filled with blubbery, lovey-dovey cuddly nonsense evolved into nagging, arguments and jealous accusations; we were *both* growing increasingly frustrated with each other.

My gut was telling me it was time to move on but I wasn't ready to let go. At the time, I felt like he was all I had. He was my security blanket and I was afraid to step out into the cold.

We had extremely different paths developing in front of us. My goal was to graduate college and get a good-paying job, then get married and start my family, the American Dream. Adrian's sails were pointed towards more ambiguous waters. Our relationship sailed through the honeymoon phase but the forecast was beginning to reveal our ship was steered straight towards the eye of a storm.

***

While at lunch one day at school, a friend tapped me on the shoulder—

"Yo, Adrian is cheating on you with his coworker."

My heart sunk. *WHAT?* Part of me didn't believe he had it in him, but if it wasn't true, why would one of his friends go out of their way to tell me? That was never something I thought I would hear. Adrian cared for me. He listened to me. He was there for me when I needed him to be. Why would he do that? Shortly after, another mutual person in our lives also told me he was cheating. If it wasn't true, why would TWO people tell me?

As soon as I came to terms with the fact that Adrian and I were now left with a dwindling sex-life, a horrendous fall-off in communication, and zero discussion of a future, I couldn't figure out what we were doing. From our ambitions to our interests, we were finally able to see we had a lot less in common than we originally thought. We cared for and loved each other, but we both knew it was over.

It was a remarkably mature break up for two individuals who were hardly adults. He had *apparently* been cheating, but since I never bothered to actually confront him about it, this remains unconfirmed, it was merely my perception of reality... I wasn't innocent either.

Adrian did help me realize one major thing, though.

LESSON #1:
Virginity doesn't matter.

The word "virgin" carries a stupid amount of weight. Virgin is a term that was developed to describe a person who has never had sex before. This concept gained a lot of attention through most religions. According to various religious beliefs, people are supposed to "remain virgins until marriage" or _forever_ or whatever. I just never understood why it was such a big deal. WHY do we _need_ to stay virgins? ...Because premarital sex is a sin? ...Because that's how a lady acts? ...Because God said so? ...Because people will lose respect? In context it seemed like it only applied to women.

If you want to lose or already lost your virginity, great! If you want to save it for marriage (another manmade concept and romantically exploited buzzword), more power to you! It's your choice, and no outside opinion should influence it. Let's evolve past that, virginity is nothing but a label that defines whether a person has had sex at least once or not. What difference does it make? Who cares?

All that matters is that we respect ourselves and each other.

Do I wish I lost my virginity to someone else? Not a chance. Adrian and I were young, naïve, and had not existed long enough on this planet to even so much as comprehend what love truly is, yet, I know we loved each other and I'll always care about him.

If I could give my virgin-self one piece of advice, it would to have sex for the right reasons, because we all deserve to be respected—*especially* by ourselves. Losing it for the sake of losing it was a dumb reason to lose it. Virginity might matter in church but has nothing to do with love. Christianity was only an influential part of my life prior to my eighteenth birthday. I abandoned the church as soon as I was old enough to abandon my mother's rule and considered myself an Agnostic or Atheist for the majority of my life.

You only get to lose your virginity once... but you can lose your virginity a million times if you have sex with a million people.

*

TWO

BEN

*"It is better to be unfaithful
than to be faithful without wanting to be."*
Brigitte Bardot

I was only single for about a month, but I was in daily contact with Ben for several *months* already. He was able have a meaningful conversation and make me ponder the world in ways I never contemplated it before. He was more curious than anyone I met during my years of parental dependency.

Ben invited me to join him for a movie, and I justified it was okay to go while I was still Adrian's girlfriend because Adrian had sex with another girl (again, I never confronted him about this). Adrian was unaware I was notified of his potentially disloyal behavior, so he didn't need to know that I was doing this.

Retaliation by imitation, *so mature.**
[*That's sarcasm. I am not proud of any of this.]

After the lights dimmed in the theatre and the previews began to roll, Ben boldly dropped some cheesy pick-up line about a rocket-ship and put his arm around me. I blushed as I looked into his eager eyes, and moments later, he pressed his face upon my own sending me to the moon and back. I melted into a pool of movie-theatre popcorn butter on my chair. We had a spark I completely missed with Adrian. Though I knew Ben for years, this was the first time that we finally connected physically.

We had both always been in the friend zone but our doors were about to be open at the same time. He was someone I felt a deeper connection to—never had I felt so intellectually matched. I always left him wanting to know more.

Technology has made it both easier and harder for us to hide things from one another. Adrian ended up snooping through my social media messages (since he set up my accounts) and read through a conversation I had mentioning that Ben and I saw a movie together. When Adrian later confronted me about it, I didn't deny it but I also did not disclose any further details. Shortly after this was when we ended our relationship. *Maybe I was wrong about Adrian being the love of my life, but Ben is the one, I just know it*, I thought.

We had many of the same interests, traits, and values. Ben opened doors for me, texted me good morning and goodnight daily. We were always on an adventure, hanging out with interesting people, playing a game or learning something new. Every time we walked by a plant with flowers blossoming, He would pick one and tuck it behind my ear. I was always smiling when we were together, we just got each other. It was easy.

Naturally, we ended up having sex as well, but it was never about getting off. It was something we did either when we got too drunk or had a good day we wanted to make better. About three months after all of this started, he told me he loved me, though I loved him long before that, and I think I might have let it slip out prematurely a couple times. I still remember the night he first said it. It was a beautiful moment because it was most important to him that *he meant it,* so he waited until he did. He was wise beyond his years (and still is).

We told each other *everything*. We were young and dumb and downright inseparable. With the exception of the hours we spent at our jobs or at school, we woke up next to each other, ate together, hung out with our friends together, ~~exercised together~~ (lol, just kidding, we didn't work out), partied together, played video games together, all of it. I wanted pizza, he ordered us a pizza. He played a sport, I learned how to play it with him. We wanted to party, we either paced each other or both got hammered. We might as well be bound together by duct tape because we were basically attached at the hip anyway.

For years, Ben and I were exclusively committed to each other; he was more than just my boyfriend, he was my best friend. It was an incredibly peaceful and loving relationship, but we literally spent every waking and sleeping second together as soon as I moved out of my parents' house into a room from Craigslist. Because of Ben, I learned a lot about what living with someone is like because I slept over at his place pretty much every night. We had disagreements here and there, as any couple does, but we talked about why we had the differences in the first place. I believed our relationship was perfect, but it was far from it. Those were my selective memories.

I was dependent on him for my happiness, the most unhealthy mindset to have: emotional dependence. He once went on vacation for a week and I cried the entire time he was away because I didn't know how to be alone.

Spending all my time and energy with Ben was distracting me from school and my grades were suffering. I was told I needed to graduate from college if I ever wanted to be successful because that's the narrative pushed by my parents (and the rest of society). I already found the guy I wanted to get married to (Ben), so all we needed to do was take the next step. After several wonderful years together, I was positive marriage was where we were heading. Getting married and bearing children was my purpose as a woman; it was the only future I ever committed to wanting since I was a little girl playing with dolls on my bedroom floor and toy cars outside in the dirt.

I had few female friends growing up; along with my sister of course, who is my friend by default, but the rest of the people I spent time with were primarily male. While other girls at my school were interested in shopping for jeans that cost $100, I was trying to figure out how to make the existing holes in my jeans look like they were designed to be that way so I didn't have to give up my favorite pair of pants. Other girls liked watching their boyfriends play in the Friday night game against our rival school, I liked throwing a football with the guys after school in the middle of the street. Other girls gossiped about who's brother they wanted to smash, I was playing the latest Super Smash Bros. video game with their brothers. Now I finally understand why I didn't have a lot of female friends growing up—I had virtually nothing in common with them.

During the days I was unable to spend time with Ben, I was hanging out with other guys because all girls did was whine and gossip and it drove me nuts. I enjoyed spending my time around opposite sex platonic (nonsexual!) friends because guys do what they want and don't waste time complaining. I was too naïve to realize most of them had other intentions when it came to their relationship with me specifically. Ben broke down to me one day when I gave my number to someone we ran into together, like *right in front of him*. I felt awful. I genuinely had no idea why it hurt him so much because I didn't have any intention of being with that guy, but he helped me understand how he felt and I never did it again.

I stopped spending so much time with all my male friends for the remaining time that we were together except for those I had work or class with. This also meant that I wasn't doing as much because I didn't have many preexisting female friends. I loved Ben and wanted him to feel more secure in our relationship so I let go of a lot of people. Things were calm for a while.

As time went on, we grew too comfortable—so comfortable that we stopped leaving the house and kept our sweatpants on all day long. We were stagnant and agitated by just about every aspect of our lives. We were sleeping in every morning and wasting the daylight rotting on the couch like forgotten potatoes. Our relationship was a long, straight road through the desert; I needed twists and turns, a change of scenery, a pitstop, something, *anything*. I was falling asleep at the metaphorical wheel of my life. I was bored. I started developing a drinking problem to keep things interesting and a strong curiosity for other drugs. Ben already tried a lot of them, why shouldn't I?

I contemplated whether or not I was making enough progress to achieve my life goals. Was Ben going to be a part of them? If we got married, would it jump start the rest of our lives together and make things interesting again? I never asked him because I just always assumed everyone wanted the same thing in life—the American Dream. What I neglected to realize was Ben's plan for the future was vastly different than my own, just as Adrian's was. After years of getting to know each other, we never had a serious conversation about the future long-term; we were too young. All I really knew was that we both feared raising children because of our childhoods.

Marriage and a family were absent from his radar at that moment in time. We were in no position to contemplate those things anyways; we were still kids ourselves. Years later I realized how foolish I was when he reminded me I wanted to be married with kids by twenty-five. Ha!

He loved me and I loved him, but we wanted different things. I prioritized my desire for marriage and the chance of finding them above Ben himself. Relationships are when two people choose to fight together for the same thing. If there was no future for "us," why were we choosing to stay together in the present? Were we both clinging on to the comfort of our familiar past? Did we both fear the unknown and being alone?

We were nothing but young adults lacking direction and ambition. We were settling in the highly dangerous "comfort zone." I was curious to know what else was out there and growing restless.

***

One sunny, spring afternoon, we were marathon watching reruns of *How I Met Your Mother* on TV when my phone vibrated on the nightstand next to his bed.

1 New Text Message

This message wasn't from just anyone, it was from another boy I knew most of my life—*my childhood crush*. Ben obviously didn't appreciate that this guy was texting me, but I didn't see any issue with it. I had no idea why he was reaching out to me; nothing ever happened between us during the decade I spent drooling over his existence, but I felt the dopamine rushing through my body just seeing his name appear on the screen of my phone. I would never disrespect Ben by pursuing someone else, but this was an instance of someone pursuing me. Responding felt harmless at the time.

It's not that another boy was texting me that upset Ben, but rather the fact that I *wanted* to respond in the first place. He couldn't comprehend why I had any business messaging this random dude back, and I had no intent of informing Ben that this guy was running laps around the track of my mind. He had been for years.

Texting is cheating just as much as kissing or sleeping with someone else; in fact, *it's arguably worse*. Cheating is determined by intention. The action disregards the feelings of another. When I was handing out my number to guys it was totally innocent because I had no intention of dating them, it was a friendship-only thing. However, this was the first time I was interested in a person that wasn't Ben. Any form of connection with someone is a building block for something more if you allow it to be, regardless of whether it be emotional, mental or physical. Cheating is not one single action, it is the ignorance of the truth—the truth being that love is not present within ourselves. I was afraid of being alone and the only way I would walk away from Ben would be if there was another patch of grass. Peeking through the hole in the fence led me to believe the lawn was pretty green on the other side, but I didn't find out until I actually hopped over.

After years of sharing Ben's bed and a zero percent chance of ever making a baby in it, I didn't see the future anymore. At that point, all we were doing was laying around, watching TV and eating. My weight was greater than it had ever been in my entire life. We never went out adventuring anymore. We never wanted to see *anyone*, there was always an excuse to stay in. Neither of us were making any effort to fix our habits or change our behavior. The relationship grew too comfortable; thus we became bored and boring. During the final months, we *both* stopped trying; it wasn't *only* me.

My crush was now the one sending me "good morning" texts and I was hiding them from Ben despite waking up next to him. Now I was convinced that my relationship with Ben was the thing making me unhappy and preventing me from exploring a world I so desperately wanted to experience. I believed this new boy would fix those problems.

Change is the only constant in life, but with us, there was no change, everything was always the same so I felt compelled to change the constant. After work one day, I built up the courage to pull the trigger; it was now or never. I drove over to Ben's house and ended things because we didn't have a long-term future. He wanted change, too, but I wanted him to change his mind about kids and marriage; something I simply cannot ask for. I couldn't help him to understand why I was ending this thing now, like *today*, at this point in time. Why wouldn't I let him try?

I didn't tell him the truth. I wanted things to work out with my crush who was holding his door open for me. I made up my mind. I learned my lesson about physical cheating before we even started dating, but had yet to understand that cheating takes many forms. It doesn't matter *how* the overlap happens (a kiss, intercourse, texting flirtatiously or lying about who you're spending time with, etc.), if the intention is to prioritize a future with someone else above the person you chose in the first place, it's cheating.

LESSON #2:
Cheating is never the answer.

The *Merriam-Webster* dictionary definition of *cheat* is "to deprive of something valuable by the use of deceit or fraud." As I mentioned before, cheating is not limited to physical unfaithfulness; it takes many forms.

A cheater *believes* that another person will make them happy, albeit temporarily, hence why they need another person to give them attention or rub skin against. And then another. And another.... Does it ever stop? How does a person break the cycle? What's the purpose of a relationship if the people in it aren't even interested in being with each other?

"They" say "once a cheater, always a cheater," but I beg to differ. It is actually quite easy not to cheat. I made a promise to myself that I would never physically cheat again on a boyfriend after kissing Ben before ending things with Adrian, but at the time I did not comprehend emotional cheating. Going to the movies with another boy when I had an exclusive boyfriend was a major no-no regardless of whether or not he kissed me. Texting my crush while still with Ben is arguably a bigger issue. My biggest struggle existed in my fear of having sex with only one person for the rest of my life, and I know for a fact I am not the only one with this anxiety. Many men I was involved with had this same concern about their future. Why do those of us whom have slept with multiple individuals fear no one person will be able to meet our "needs?"

I get it now, but I want you to understand, too.

This is still just the beginning.

We must close doors before we open new ones. It isn't love if you allow someone you care about to hold their door open for you while you're out there knocking on other doors. Multiple open doors means air is flowing between rooms, fluctuating the temperature, mixing scents, and allowing for noise pollution. It is easy to recognize when a person you love is involved with someone else if you unconditionally love them because their behavior will contradict itself, just like mine did in almost every chapter of this book. Ben knew something was wrong the second I got that initial message from my crush.

When you eat dinner, do you set your food down, load up a new plate; eat that one, then return to your original plate? No way. You'll most likely be full and the first plate is going to be cold by the time you get back to it. Why on Earth would we do that *to people*?

At least finish what's on the first plate before walking away.

That is beyond messed up.

*

THREE

CALEB

*"If they substituted the word 'Lust' for 'Love' in the
popular songs it would come nearer the truth."*
Sylvia Plath

It is impossible to pinpoint exactly when and where my feelings for Caleb originated. I had that butterfly-in-the-stomach feeling every time I saw him from the first time until the last. I would never admit that to him as a googley-eyed teenager but now we were both single and in our twenties, no braces nor pimples, and things between us were finally about to escalate.

For nearly a decade, he was my fixation. I found many boys to be attractive, but Caleb was on a completely different level; he brought about a feeling within me limited to only a select group of men. Each time I gazed into his eyes, I forgot everything else. Let's pick up our story immediately after I broke up with Ben…

And I mean *immediately* after walking out Ben's front door.

***

Tears were streaming down my face. I sprinted back to my car, put the key in the ignition and slammed my forehead on the top of the steering wheel. Was I out of my mind? Did I make the right decision? Had I just thrown away the best thing that ever happened to me? I took a deep breath and focused on calming myself down. *Breathe in, breathe out. In, out.* Again. *In, out. Just breathe…*

Once the panic subsided, I drove straight over to none other than Caleb's house to say "Hi;" which was perhaps not my finest decision. As you might imagine, I wanted for Caleb to want to be my boyfriend now. It would be the perfect fairy tale ending to the love story I dreamt up when we were teenagers. I was infatuated in the unhealthiest of ways.

I stood at the edge of his garage while he was inside working on his car, shirtless. Every cell in my body wanted nothing more than for him to grab me, push me up against the wall and passionately press his lips upon mine...

Alas, this was nothing but an innocent conversation; I was only there to say "Hi." It was his choice to hold interest in me, for whatever reason that might be. It had to be his decision, not mine, and there was nothing I could do that would change that, and I was aware. During this brief interaction I did not inform him that I was now single, I wanted him to find out on his own.

We have been taught to listen to our feelings because that's who we are, but also, to ignore our feelings because they cause us to do things that are irrational. Feelings are a combined result our natural instincts and our past experiences. We all have them. Emotions and feelings are influenced by the past, present, and future, by dreams and history and imagination. We don't always have control over the way we feel, but we do have control over the way in which we choose to respond.

Because I failed to find my "soulmate" twice, I wanted to make sure that this thing with Caleb was for real, that he wanted me just as much as I wanted him. Would Caleb connect the dots and discover that I was single? What would he say? Would he think I was crazy? Would he trust me? Did he already know and not say anything? It felt like an eternity, I was both terrified and excited for him to learn. He continued texting me for weeks and we were getting to know each other on a different level than we had throughout our lifetime of coexistence.

One evening I *finally* got the message I was waiting for:

You broke up with Ben?

That night, he invited me over to hang out with him and his friends. This was it, he was welcoming me into his life. Things intensified quickly, and by things, I mean our blood alcohol levels. Before I knew it, I was a few beers deep, feeling fuzzy, flirty and fabulous. I glanced at my phone and noticed the clock was closing in on midnight, but I wasn't ready to leave and he wanted me to stay a bit longer as well. I was ecstatic.

Eventually, the group of friends stopped drinking and one by one, they headed home until Caleb and I were the only two individuals remaining at the table. I kid you not, we talked on that patio until the sun came up the next morning. We couldn't find a good place to end our conversation. We talked about the past, the present, *and* the future. We talked about our favorite ice cream flavors and pizza toppings. We talked about jobs and kids and school. We talked about outer space. We shared stories about our upbringings. We talked about marriage and Jesus and how pointless promise rings are. We were on different ladders climbing at the same pace, but I was already losing my footing and we hadn't even shared our first kiss yet.

As soon as the sun peaked over the mountain, it hit me that I didn't have my uniform for work, so I *really* had to leave. He walked me to my car and the moment I dreamt of for years finally happened.

He kissed me!

It was the Fourth of July in my frontal cortex. I wasn't ready for it and immediately felt the explosion of feelings consume me as dopamine rushed through my entire body like light illuminates a room upon flipping the switch.

If "love" was for real, this was it. I was sure of it.

***

"May I please get a large, quad-shot soy latte?"

I recognized that voice and glanced in the camera screen to Caleb's cheerful smile. I signaled my coworker to pass the call along to me.

"Good morning, Caleb!"

"Hey babe." The enormous grin on my face had all my coworkers thinking I won the lottery. *He called me "babe" and visited me at work!* Was he falling for me as hard as I was for him? Our chat was brief and ended in plans to see each other that evening. *What a perfect man,* I thought to myself as I waved him off. Would today be the day things really started to heat up between us? Would this be the day we make things official?

I showed up to his house at sundown and he greeted me with a passionate kiss in the doorway. Just being in his presence had my blood pumping through my veins faster than normal. The closer

I got, the closer I wanted to be. I changed into my swimsuit and we took the plunge into the steamy hot tub. I knew where this was going and I'm sure you do, too.

We spent many nights together in that hot tub. Every once in a while, he made me dinner. He visited me at work. He texted me first thing every morning. He shared his secrets with me. He treated me like a princess. He was everything I wanted... but he never asked me to be his girlfriend, so I was still single. He thought labels were dumb. I agreed that labels weren't important to me either, but here's the kicker—*that was a lie.* Why would I be dishonest about that? It's what I thought he wanted to hear. (People pleasing...)

All our other friends and family were in *labeled* relationships. Was I doing something wrong? The other two guys I had sex with called me their girlfriend, what was Caleb waiting for? Did he not like me as much as I thought he did? The more I thought about it, the more I panicked; and the more I questioned his intentions, the less I was able to focus on him. A week before my birthday, contact from Caleb abruptly stopped.

One day passed... nothing. Another day... nothing. Day three slipped by and still not a single text from him. I was confused. What the heck was happening?

> *Hi! I'm having a party Friday for my birthday,*
> *let me know if you can make it!*

I anxiously hit the SEND button. But again, radio silence.

Was my phone broken? I re-sent the same message, convincing myself I wasn't desperate and that there was clearly just an issue with one of our phones. I was trying to hold myself together because it was clear the connection and communication between us vanished.

What the hell happened?

Three days passed. Nothing. On day four, I stared disheartened at the ceiling, half-asleep.

BZZZT.

I was snapped out of my morning slumber by the vibration of my phone under my pillow. A fat smile stretched across my face—it was him. *FINALLY.*

Heyy! I'm not sure if I'm going to be able to make it to your party, but I should be able to! ☺

I immediately began overanalyzing each word, from the number of Y's in "Hey" to the happy punctuation. *He's still going to try to make it, that's good, so he probably will, right? Yeah, totally. He even smiled. Oh the smile on his face. He's so cute… Why can't I stop thinking about him? Will he ask me to be his girlfriend tonight? He's going to be there, right? Totally.*

I was so insecure I was seeking assurance from anyone who would listen. I wasn't thinking for myself. Everything I did was calculated and based on what other people told me to do, or the exact opposite. I didn't want to respond to his message since it literally took him <u>DAYS</u> to acknowledge my invitation, but I also really wanted to see him. I told myself I would get back to him later.

I threw off the covers and plunged my feet into my slippers.

Time to get to work. Time equals money and a paycheck doesn't earn itself.

***

"Hey! It's me."

There he was, sitting in the drive-thru prepared to grab some caffeine and say "hello" after nearly disappearing completely. We chatted for a brief moment as not to hold up the line too long. He waved goodbye as he drove off and with this, I was sure he would be at my party. I couldn't wait to see him and introduce him to all my friends. He was my "soulmate," I just knew it. I needed to slow down; I was practically charging a brick wall at a hundred miles an hour without brakes.

The evening of my party arrived and I spent the entire night staring at the clock and checking my phone for messages, anxiously watching the hands inch closer to midnight. I began to freak out. *Where is he?* My friends urged me to stop worrying and have a good time, but I could only focus my attention on one person—

Caleb.

Midnight struck and it occurred to me that he wasn't coming. Why was I so invested in his presence? Dozens of my closest friends were here for me, yet I could only think about the one that wasn't. I spared my friends the depressed version of myself as they shoved my first legal shots into my hands and one by one, I tipped them back down my throat. The more I had, the easier it was to evade the mental state of loneliness. Caleb's absence may not have ruined the remainder of the night, but the alcohol certainly did.

***

Before I knew it, it was the next afternoon.

The early hours of the morning were a blur. To my understanding, I achieved a level of intoxication that was potentially deadly, and I would prefer not to reach that level of mortality again. I learned the toilet makes a dreadful pillow and allowing chunky, multicolored vomit to dry on a pair of new heels will destroy them forever.

Waiting on my phone was a new text message from Caleb, apologizing deeply for missing the festivities of the night prior. It shouldn't come as a surprise that he didn't attend. He was not my boyfriend and he was not interested in labels, we discussed that. I never told him what I wanted or admitted I had true feelings for him, so how could I expect to know if he felt the same way? We stopped communicating about the future after we swapped out our time talking for physical acts. I didn't want to pressure him into a relationship which is why I never initiated the DTR (Define The Relationship) conversation in the first place. I feared that if I did, I would lose him forever.

With my current understanding, I believe there are many reasons Caleb vanished. I completely lost confidence in myself, doubted my every move, and was dependent on him (at the time) for my own happiness; a burden too heavy for anyone to carry.

He wasn't getting what he wanted or needed. How could I give that to him? I had no idea what that even was. I didn't understand at the time; I ignored all the signs and heard only what I wanted to hear. I cried for *months*. There was so much undeniable chemistry and a strong connection between us when it started, but it was now reduced to emptiness. Did I do something wrong? Was I insane? Blind? Stupid? What initiated his abrupt change in behavior?

LESSON #3
Lust is NOT love.

It was literally day and night. There were so many questions I wanted answers to, but it was easier to blame the whole thing on myself because as far as I was concerned, he was perfect and could do no wrong. My primary thought was, *I must not be good enough.*

He was attractive, had a career, a car, and a supportive family. He was clever, respectful, and kind. He was outdoorsy and ambitious. He had a plan and another plan for how he was going to get there. I thought I was in love with him, but I was so blinded by the idea of being with him, I wasn't even paying attention to what he was telling me. He was filling a void in my life, but it wasn't "love." It was merely what I thought love was.

I spent every waking moment of my day thinking about him. Even my friends were going crazy because I wouldn't shut up about him. I was in withdrawal. I had zero control over my emotions.

There was *one* thing that likely contributed to the abrupt change in *both* our behavior around the time he started distancing himself; a dreadful, *unconscious* blunder of mine that haunted me for years and messed me up in more ways than just this one… and I never connected the dots on any of this until I wrote this. I hope that my experience in the next chapter will spare other young adults the indecency that I underwent during my first few experimental years with alcohol. Mind you, we were all very, very young and very naïve. My intention in sharing the next two stories with you is not to throw anyone under the bus, but to instead help others learn through my experiences.

Are you prepared to dive into some deep water?

I hope you know how to swim.

*

FOUR

DAWSON

"No one saves us but ourselves.
No one can and no one may.
We ourselves must walk the path."
Buddha

Let's backtrack to a few weeks *before* my party. Edward (a platonic friend you'll meet soon) invited me to an event one of his buddies was hosting. There would be some dudes at this party I was less familiar with, but I grew up with most of them in school. It was going to be awesome to see them all again after I originally cut contact whilst dating Ben, but I was in no way interested in anyone else that night because I was obsessed with Caleb.

About two hours before going to this party, I lost a grandparent. Caleb was there for me, literally, sitting with me on the curb outside my parents' house and talking me through it, but then I was invited to go to this party with Edward. My first mistake was choosing to go to this party in the emotional state I was in—I was a total wreck.

Before I even reached the door, I heard the screams and chants of college kids. Everyone was playing beer pong, getting high and telling stories around the fire pit, laughing and sincerely just having a jolly-good time. Soon I was on their level, and the sheer amount of fun I was having was exactly what I longed for. I drank myself into the ground; hammered is an understatement.

After too many beers, one guy had this bright idea—

"Let's go graffiti the school! We have spray paint!"

Woah! That escalated quickly, but I suppose that is to be expected from a group of rebellious drunk college kids. Those dudes took off but I had zero interest in being a part of it. By this point, I was piss drunk, sloppily walking into people and spilling my drink all over the place, but thankfully still had the integrity not to cross that legal boundary.

Everyone left the house except for me.

...And Dawson.

In fact, Dawson's pearly white smile caught my attention immediately upon walking into my life *years* prior to this night. All the other girls at school talked about how cute he was, and for some reason, *he was interested in me*. I struggled to put the pieces together. There was no denying he was dreamy; but on this particular evening he was my worst nightmare.

This is your **TRIGGER WARNING**, by the way. In the event you want to avoid this sort of stuff, you can just skip this chapter, but I suggest reading it—I keep things tasteful.

I stumbled back inside the house to pour myself a glass of water and use the restroom. I don't know how much I drank that night, but I do know it was too much. I experienced "blackout drunk" a few times before this; however, I was never *alone*. Not like this. I was the only girl left at this party and Edward, the platonic friend who invited me, was out spray-painting penises on a wall.

For the first time in my drinking career, no one was around to look out for me. I always had a boyfriend since I lost my virginity, but at this point in time by no means had I ever "slept around." I thought I would marry Adrian, Ben and Caleb while I was with them, and that we would live happily ever after. But life is not a fairy-tale—not in this reality anyways.

Dawson followed me inside and pushed me up against the kitchen counter from behind while I was filling up my cup with water. He turned my body around so I was facing his while he pressed his face against mine, then his hand slid into my pants.

"I don't want to do anything," I pushed him away.

"Come on, let's have a little fun. Everyone is gone."

"I just want to sleep."

He wrapped his arms around me, picked me up and carried me down the hall to a spare room with nothing but a leather sofa and a computer. He set me down in the center of the couch and the next thing I knew, my clothes were being removed.

"I don't want to do this," I held on to my pants for dear life but they ended up on the floor with everything else. Moments later, he was on top of me; one hand over my mouth and the other holding the weight of his body above mine. I couldn't push him off; I didn't stand a chance.

I just let him do it.

We were *both* heavily intoxicated, it wasn't just me. Try to stop a drunk person from doing anything they want and that alone may be one of the biggest challenges you face in life. I laid there motionless while he proceeded to get his fix. I'll spare you the remaining details because frankly, they are irrelevant. "No" was nothing but a useless two-letter word. I faded in and out of consciousness for the majority of it. (*Fortunately*.)

Then, I heard a door slam.

Voices—the remaining guys returned from their vandalism excursion and Dawson's hand returned to its original position over my mouth. I was no longer on the couch; my bare stomach was now pressed against the cold hardwood floor. I was pinned between the two dirtiest things I knew in this world at the time: the ground of a college party house and a horny drunk guy.

His friends walked by and some of them glanced in the room to see what was going on, but not a single one of them seemed to care, they kept walking. I slid back into the unconsciousness; it was safer there. Some more time passed. When I snapped back into the present moment, the entire group of guys were huddled around the computer watching something while I was still naked on the floor behind them. I was quiet for a while. I tried to say something, but it was still muffled by the palm of Dawson's hand. I curled up into a ball to shield my body from the group of guys in the room. He picked me up again, hand still covering my mouth, and relocated my body onto the couch. It was the most humiliated, helpless, and invisible I've ever felt in my life.

To this day, there is still not a single event that tops it.

***

It was five o'clock in the morning when I was capable of functioning again. The worst was over. Boys were scattered about the house on couches, some across chairs, others passed out on the floor, and one kid literally K.O.'ed on the staircase. I roamed the house and found my shoes, stopped in the bathroom, vomited profusely and got out of there. This was perhaps the second sunrise I remember since the first one just months prior with Caleb.

Alcohol was a pretty new thing for me, so I had no idea what a limit was. I didn't understand what things were going to be like as a female drinking *alone* with a bunch of guys. Plain and simple, I drank too much; there's zero excuse for that. Blaming this whole thing on Dawson wouldn't be fair because we kissed once before—though our history was innocent.

With that said, respect is something we all lose when we drink too much. Ultimately, the only thing I could have done differently to ensure this was avoided would be not attending.

This occurred before the "Consent Movement" took off. It is easy to accuse Dawson for taking advantage of me or the situation or attribute it to the alcohol for rendering us both incapable of rational decision-making, but I must take responsibility for the events that occurred in my reality as the only thing I can control is myself. Thanks to how much alcohol I drank, I wasn't even able to do that.

LESSON #4:
You are the only person who will always have your back.

Seems like common sense, right? As I mentioned before, I make a lot of mistakes, which I'm sure you probably agree at this point, but I'm'ma keep on makin' 'em. I was an incredibly irresponsible twenty year old when this occurred. If you don't know what your limits are, figure that out pronto. In a safe place. With people you trust. Alcohol is *factually* poison and brings out toxic behavior in its consumers. Coincidence? Nah. I don't believe in those. Everything happens for a reason.

When we are young, drinking is great because it helps us forget about how hard we are all trying to fit in. We get to be the person we want to be without fear of what other people think. When we are older, a major reason we drink is because we begin to realize fitting in sucks and we want to escape it. For those who believe they *need* alcohol, it is not only the solution to life's problems, but also the cause.

When I arrived that night, I had zero intention of hooking up with anyone—I was invested in Caleb—but I drank too much. I asked Dawson to stop, but I *reciprocated* his initial kiss! If I wanted to be with Caleb so bad, why would I do that? It doesn't make sense. In my drunken state it was practically an instinct because we'd kissed before. Dawson, in turn, likely interpreted my reciprocation as consent, and can you blame him? Had he been sober, I'm positive he would handle the situation as differently as I would. The whole scenario would be avoidable had we not been belligerent.

I believe today's rape culture supports women's throwing around of the "R" word regardless of the circumstances; the events leading to how it happened and whether or not drugs or alcohol were involved. Aren't we all a bit to blame? It takes two, after all.

At the end of the day, <u>you</u> are ultimately the <u>only</u> person who has your best interests at heart, and though weakening ourselves with alcohol might be fun, we must accept the risks of losing self-control—I've been drugged before, too, which is something you literally have no idea of when it is happening to you (but that's not a story you'll hear in this book).

Tears were still streaming down my face when I pulled up to my house. I wanted nothing more than to curl up in my bed, squeeze my stuffed animals, and scream into my pillow at the top of my lungs. Never in my life had I felt so alone, used, and unloved. I tried to remain as quiet as possible as to not wake up my housemates as I entered through the front door. I crawled up the stairs, down the hall and to my room and grabbed the handle. It didn't budge.

That's strange, I thought. *Don't panic, just grab the spare key.*

My roommate and I never locked the door, so this was unusual. After obtaining the key from the kitchen downstairs and unlocking the door, I swung my bedroom door open to find my roommate sleeping in her bed and *her boyfriend passed out in mine*—a true Goldilocks affair! I grabbed my sweatpants and sprinted back down the hall to the bathroom where I turned on the shower, sat naked in the tub and cried. First, my body was taken advantage of; and now, even my own bed had a strange man in it.

When I returned, the bear was still snuggled up inside my blankets as his face swam in a slippery puddle of drool on my pillow. I collected my work uniform, returned to my car, and cried myself to sleep there. Everything that could go wrong was going wrong. I had no self-respect, and shortly after this was when things with Caleb started to crumble. Could *this* be what rock bottom feels like?

Oof. I had a long way to fall...

Things get worse before they get better.

*

FIVE

EDWARD

"People go through so much pain trying to avoid pain."
Neil Strauss

Edward was someone I knew for a long time. We played with toy cars in the dirt, hopped fences, rode bikes off trails and smoked weed just about everywhere we could. He encouraged me to push boundaries because he was pushing them, too. No one knew me quite the way Edward did during my teenage years.

After breaking up with Ben, we started hanging out more than we had in my pre-Adrian days. I knew Edward had a crush on me because people told me; but for the first time in my life I had space to allow the idea of being with him to marinate in my mind. I never considered dating him and I knew getting involved with him would destroy the dynamic of our friendship because I saw how he treated his ex, but after a summer of beach trips, fire pits, and bong hits, Edward became a greater part of my life than I expected. Would the friend-zone yield a beautiful love story after all?

We had zero romantic history. It was always platonic—I never wanted anything else. On the day he first kissed me, I still didn't want anything, but I decided to give him a shot because he was one of my closest friends. What if he was my soulmate after all? Up to this point, I was wrong about almost everything.

One afternoon while we were watching a movie on the sofa, he made his first sexual move. It felt aggressive, but after what I had been through with Dawson, "aggressive" didn't mean the same thing it once did. If I wanted to keep Edward in my life, I thought I would have to have sex with him eventually, so I figured I might as well just do it now to make him happy. A few weeks later, *BAM*. We were relationship status official, which was exactly what I thought I wanted.

We made an explosive combo; both immature, witty, and energetic. We had raunchy senses of humor, smoked loads of pot, played video games and ate way too much junk food. We were both wildly competitive and hated losing more than almost anything else. I knew from the first sexual advance he made that we were a match made in hell—and I was right.

***

The descent began with a promise... or rather, a promise *ring*.

Edward knew an awful lot about me, but for some reason decided my opinion on this topic wasn't relevant enough to have a conversation about before moving forward with obtaining one. I believed promise rings were ridiculous and unnecessary. Why not just go all the way and get engaged? Edward spent the entirety of dinner insisting that I wear it as a promise to him because he bought it for me. I didn't understand why I was supposed to wear it.

While he said the ring represented my commitment to him, he made it blatantly clear that it in no way meant that he was promising anything to me—I asked him to get one as well and he refused. What is the point of wearing a ring that looks like an engagement ring, but doesn't symbolize a mutual commitment to spend the rest of our lives together?

We thought we knew almost everything about each other; but apparently we were both very wrong. I could have absolutely rejected the ring but in the end, I still put it on my finger because I wanted to make him happy since it was important to him. I had more respect for Edward than I had for myself; the mindset of a true people-pleaser, and he knew it, too. I didn't know how to stand up for myself.

Love never felt this wrong.

My resentment for him grew each time I glanced at the meaningless piece of metal sparkling on my finger. The promise ring debacle and every other argument from that day forward ended the same way: he brought up the fact that I had sex with Dawson at the party he brought me to. This routinely resulted in a complete shutdown of my emotions because Edward didn't understand my story. Instead he used it against me because it elicited a reaction every time; like a kill shot. I just wanted to forget about that night forever and he consistently used it to manipulate me. He brought this up again and again and again; and how awful I was that I did that to him even though at that point in time I was not his girlfriend.

My self-esteem was so low, I believed I was unlovable, and he enforced that thought by making me feel like he was the only one out there who will take me for what I was... *A SLUT.* Even my mother was guilty of using the term against me during high school before I ever had my first kiss. Though hardly an adult now, I already had a handful of lovers, exhibits A through E. Sexual partner count is simply just a number. Like age, it can only go up.

Stereotypically, men are praised for their sexual triumphs. It is common to see men sleeping around and high-fiving each other in movies for their accomplishments in the bedroom. On the other hand, women were labeled with derogatory terms. How can it be so that men are treated as though they accomplished something, but women like they failed? This concept is ludicrous. *We're all doing the same damn thing—It takes two!*

After about a year of being in a relationship, he started telling me "[my] future husband is going to be extremely lucky one day because of [him]." Why was he talking about my future like he wasn't going to be in it? After wearing the promise ring he so desperately wanted me to wear? Now the only person who loved me didn't even see me in their future. I was confused.

He repeatedly reminded me how important it was for us to be naked around each other all the time. "Sex is ninety percent of a relationship" was his tagline; he recited it almost daily. If that didn't achieve what he wanted, he guilt-tripped me with the Dawson situation again, or called me a lesbian. My self-esteem was so low, when he tried to break up with me, I *begged* him not to leave me. His rebuttal was that if we stay together, he wanted to be in an open relationship so he could have sex with other people.

Edward is the only person I was ever involved with who yelled at me. One argument ended when he told me whatever I was "feeling" doesn't matter because I was his girlfriend so I needed to have sex with him whenever he wanted it. It felt like I was being stabbed and he was twisting the knife while it was buried deep in my skin. Oh, how my heart aches for that girl.

Edward was right about one thing, though; my future husband *is* going to be lucky—only, not for the reasons by which he intended when he made such a claim.

No matter how many times I tried to explain my feelings to him, I was unable to break through. On an almost regular basis, he told me he wanted to "go on a break." (Fun fact: "go on a break" is generally synonymous with "hook up with other people.") It happened to loads of my friends and I was not about to be fooled. I told him if he wanted to break up, he could also count on not getting back together, and I even broke that promise to myself by the time it was all said and done.

He later revealed that he gave me the promise ring to prevent other people from hitting on me because he didn't trust me around other guys—a wildly hypocritical statement considering he hit on almost every girl he came into contact with. He slapped my friend's butts, cat-called random chicks even when I was standing right next to him, and spent hours of his free time consuming porn. There were several instances I woke up in the morning to him actually attempting to thrust himself inside me.

I never told him how I felt about any of it. I never told him my friends hated having their butts slapped or that cat-calling is not a respectful way to communicate with women. I accepted a promise ring I didn't want. Most importantly, I lacked the strength to tell him I felt violated when he tried to have sex with me while I was sleeping. I was petrified of what people would think of me for jumping from relationship to relationship if I left him, so I stayed.

Our relationship was the knife that kept on cutting.

Why was I holding on to the side with the blade?

***

One night I remember particularly well—we were chilling outside smoking in the street with a few friends. Edward and I were debating the topic of being kicked in the groin. He alleged that if women were kicked there, it does not hurt. While I imagine a groin kick likely does hurt men more than it hurts women due to their extremities, receiving a kick anywhere on the body inflicts pain. Duh. Edward felt inclined to find out for himself.

Guess what he had the balls to do?

Before I knew it, I received a flying foot of force between my legs. He literally kicked me in the sandwich.

"WHAT THE F***?" I shrieked.

One of his friends pushed him to the ground.

What was he thinking? He obviously wasn't; and *neither was I*—I should've dumped him right then and there but my lack of self-respect and fear of being alone were so overpowering I still thought being with him was better than being alone. I brainwashed myself into believing I was worthless. I was stuck in a mindset where I felt it was my duty to bend over backwards for my lover's every desire. My dignity was depleted. His friends were the only ones that witnessed how he treated me; I was so blind, not even I could see the problem. Edward led me to believe that emotionless sex was a requirement for a relationship.

He used to be my closest friends.

***

"Why *are* you still with Edward?" A mutual friend asked me as we sat smoking cigarettes in the cold.

It was a good question; I didn't even know anymore. The list of pros and cons consisted almost entirely of cons. Aside from my distorted understanding of "love" and the history we shared, what was left? I was alone whether or not I was with Edward. He was a major part of my life for as long as I could remember but I didn't know who he was anymore, nor did I have a clue who I had become.

Thankfully my friends finally started to see what was happening and took the time to help me free myself since I wouldn't be honest or open about what was really going on. They exposed Edward for being an emotional vampire. His highly toxic behavior sucked all my blood and the veins to my heart were completely dry.

***

On New Year's Day, I woke up earlier than all my roommates, Edward still snoozing in my bed. I knew he would be there for another four or five hours considering how much he had to drink the night before. I slid my toes into my fuzzy slippers, wrapped myself in a heavy blanket, and waddled outside to the patio. The prior night's party was so epic, there was no chance anyone else would be awake. I wanted to be alone anyways; it felt better than being in my bed with someone I felt alone next to.

However, not even five minutes after I sat down, the door knob turned. To my surprise, my roomie and close friend sat down next to me and handed me a cup of coffee. We lit our cigarettes in silence and stared at the empty bottles, cans, confetti, and fold-up chairs that littered our backyard. I never needed to explain to her what I was feeling, she just knew. Unexpectedly, she presented me with a proposition that would forever change the course of my life.

"How do you feel about accounting? You should come in for an interview at my office. We're hiring." I had no degree, no experience, and no idea what an office job even entailed, but opportunity was knocking and I had to give it a shot. To my astonishment, I got the job, but that's a story for some other time. I was finally about to escape this town and the people binding me to it for good.

I packed up my things and never looked back; it's impossible to catch me once I'm gone. I broke up with Edward and returned his promise ring, and he continued to bombard me with phone calls and text messages for months. He told me I would never find the kind of love we had with anyone else. He was right—I never will; nor do I ever want to.

LESSON #5:
It's better to be alone than in a toxic relationship.

We teach others how to treat us. This truth is simple, yet so often we too strongly desire a relationship itself with no regard for the quality of it, which is far more important. Tolerating an abusive partner ultimately does more harm than anything else to both individuals. Someone may tell you they love you, but what does that actually mean? What does love mean to them?

The single most disturbing part about abusive partners is that when we are with one, we usually don't see it this way. When we succumb ourselves to toxic behavior for enough time, it becomes our new normal. We are voluntarily laying in the middle of the road waiting for cars to run us over. The good news is that upon recognizing toxic behavior for what it truly is, it's incredibly easy to free ourselves from it. All we must do is stand up and get out of the road.

Because I tolerated Edward's behavior, I taught him it was okay to treat me such way. I was unable to stand up for myself nor find the strength within myself to walk away. I was the one who decided to lay down in the middle of the road in the first place.

After we finally broke up, I went rogue. I, too, now believed sex was the most important component of a relationship as it was the only thing that distinguished a significant other from the rest of the guys in my life. There was only one thing I disagreed with him on which was quantity. NINETY PERCENT?! No way. But if it wasn't ninety, what was it? Fifty? Fifteen? Five? We were having sex almost every day, occasionally more than once, but no matter what, it was never enough for him. *How could that be possible?*

***

Commuting from my hometown to my new job was torturous but every mile of distance I put between Edward and myself was worth it. It kept me occupied physically, emotionally, and mentally. Edward was evolving into a bitter memory while an extraordinary seed of confidence blossomed within me. It was hard learning to live without him, but grew easier with each passing day.

For the first time in a long time, I felt free.

I can't help but wonder where Edward learned his behavior. I don't think Edward is a bad person, he likely endured his own fair share of emotional trauma just like me and you. We all have it in us to be good people; even those who do things that appear evil to the rest.

Love and sex do crazy things to our brains and are major reasons a lot of people do irrational things. He was dangerously addicted to sex and though I was, too, I was unable to enjoy it with him for some reason. I completely zoned out every time we were naked, much like I did with Dawson. To protect my feelings from further trauma, I constructed an emotional wall and topped it off with electrified barbed wire so that if anyone else tried to get close to me, they would be electrocuted before they even knew what was on the other side.

The rest of this book is about the people who tried; and almost all of them were stopped dead in their tracks. I was on a suicide mission to find my one true love; inflicting pain and uncertainty in the life of anyone who crossed paths with me. Wounds not tended to with care will not recover properly, if at all.

My unaddressed wounds bled for years.

*

SIX

FELIX

"May your choices reflect your hopes, not your fears."
Nelson Mandela

During one of the darkest times in my life, this guy was there to extend a helping hand to pull me out just enough to see the light again. I won't reminisce on Felix for too long, but he was a friend of someone else I dated, thus perpetually off limits...

Until now.

Following my big move to the city, Felix occasionally reached out to check in and see how I was doing, and after a brief exchange of text messages we'd continue about our separate lives. After months of occasional drop ins to my inbox, it felt like he wasn't just checking-in, it started to feel like a little *more*. We were getting deep (in conversation, that is). Felix was the last untouched cookie from the jar of my past life. I was ready to frolic in my new playground, *the big city*, but what if Felix was the one after all those times he was there for me?

I invited Felix over to my place and for one of the first times in our lives, it was just the two of us. Now that we were both single, potential for something more to happen between us existed. Soon after, I visited him and we chatted around a bonfire in his yard, smoking weed and laughing all night long. When I was with him, I forgot about my ex.

After a few evenings together, he took a chance.

He kissed me.

Soon we were going out for sushi and to the movies; we were even having sleepovers. Our relationship was like the Easter Egg you find in the house a couple days later with the treat still inside; a sweet surprise. I never comprehended he was into me like that. I struggled to make peace with this because I cared too much about what people would think if I were to date my ex's friend, nor did I want anything to do with their friendship. One of the major reasons I moved to the city was to escape my hometown and the people in it!

I connected Felix with a few of my own friends over the years, who each had their own flings with him, the details of which were not of my concern. It didn't bother me; the past is the past. Mine already wasn't pretty. Thankfully, the past is why we are the people we are in the present.

Felix was sitting next to me on my patio, clouds of smoke floating around our heads while we laughed and discussed what the next years of our life were going to look like. Like me, he was about to embark on an adventure that would change the course of his forever. He created a plan for himself; a building block for climbing towards his future goals. I admired his ambition; as it inspired me to do the same.

For a moment, I truly believed that maybe, just maybe, he was the one I was meant to spend the rest of my life with. We both knew we would make a great couple, what was stopping us?

I continued to concentrate on the fact that he was my ex's friend and I still wanted to talk to other guys because I wasn't ready to commit. "They" say when you know, you know, and even though I loved Felix, I knew I wasn't ready to be with only him for the rest of my life. Months went by of our undiscussed fling until one day Felix threw me a curve ball—

"Where is this going?"

I wanted to skyrocket out of bed and run for the mountains. I had no idea what to say. Something was missing and it had absolutely nothing to do with Felix.

"I... I don't know." I held my breath. I was at a loss.

In that moment I realized I was stringing him along; I was unable to be what he wanted. I never asked him where this was going, and I didn't ask him because I knew the answer was nowhere. I was holding him back from finding her (which he since has). We laid there in silence and stared blankly at the ceiling. I contemplated what I could say to make things better, I never wanted to lead him on. I thought I was ready for a relationship but I wasn't even close. After so many failed attempts at choosing the right person, I doubted my own ability to make choices.

I mean, *how would that work out for us?* He was about to embark on an epic career change that would take him far, far away from here and I was dependent on having someone present, *physically.* I struggled to wrap my mind around a long-distance relationship. He would be gone for who knows how long and sex was a checklist item in a relationship for me. There's no sex with long distance. Pessimistic thoughts swirled around in my brain. *What would my ex do? What would people think?* I believed everyone would judge me and I had yet to free myself from the burden of caring what other people think. I was up against more than I was willing to take on.

Without another word, he leapt out of my bed and rummaged around on the floor for his clothes. He didn't understand how I felt or what I wanted but I didn't know how to explain that to him because I didn't know either. I was closed off. I cared about him, I loved him, and all I wanted to do was make him happy, but we wanted different things.

We gave each other a hug—a different kind than most. It was one of those hugs when you know you're going to be hugging a person for the last time. I had this same hug before with a few others and I would go on to have them with many more before writing this—it's the extended, intimate, tremendously tight embrace of mutual melancholy. It is the knowing that there is not a future but still having love for each other; the final moments of a dream. It is knowing this is the absolute goodbye. We both knew it.

"Please let me know when you get home." I managed to say as he walked out my front door.

He nodded and kissed me on the cheek. "You are an amazing girl, don't ever forget that. You deserve the best and you will find it someday." I reciprocated his message and bid him farewell, holding back my tears. I am so grateful for him.

LESSON #6
Love is NOT a feeling. Love is a choice.

Just because we did not end up together does not mean we did or do not love each other; sometimes the best thing we can do when we love someone is to let them go. I chose to love Felix, and in this case, that meant letting him go so he would be able to find what he was looking for. I was a distraction to him, I did not realize how he felt about me until he brought up the future.

We are presented with opportunity for love more often than we recognize, but because we are by nature easily distracted by lust or consumed by fear, we struggle to focus enough to see love for what it is. Every single person in the world has the *choice* to love whomever they choose to love. Love Is a choice and a mindset, not a physical sensation or emotional state. The decision is truly ours; it is not predetermined by a higher being, our sexuality, our feelings, friends or parents.

I *choose* to love my family, I *choose* to love my friends, I *choose* to love my coworkers, I *choose* to love complete strangers, I *choose* to love my exes, and I *choose* even to love people who do not love me in return. Regardless of whatever life throws at me, loving others is a major part of what makes life worth living. If we have the choice to love whomever we want, we must understand what it truly means to love and again, I was far too naïve to conceptualize this.

Felix and I were both mature enough to understand that our fling ran its course and we reached our expiration date. We shared a deep connection but because our futures were not aligned it was best to extract ourselves from each other's lives. We reached the crossing point, but our lines just weren't paralleled.

Life in the big city was providing me with a playground full of new dating options, yet here I was still playing catch in my own backyard. I still needed to take off my clothes in public, do drugs with strangers and skinny dip in the ocean. I needed to *really* feel rock bottom. I needed to have sex on balconies and afterparty with football players. I needed to see what a strip club was like, I needed to get in trouble with the law. Most importantly, I really needed to have my heart broken so I could feel the pain I inflicted on many others. I needed to experience everything because growing up in a strict and sheltered household left me feeling like I experienced nothing.

I chose to live my new, adventurous life instead of walk down a traditional path with Felix. I had no idea what it was like to be alone because I was always able to fill the male void in my life relatively quickly. I didn't even realize it, but he was filling that void for me so I wasn't in withdrawal. The longer we remained in each other's lives, the longer we wouldn't be able to fully give ourselves to anyone else. I promised myself I wouldn't tell any more boys I loved them unless I was positive I felt that way, the question was— how would I ever be sure?

I now choose to love everyone because I have a far better understanding of what it means than I did at the time these things happened. Love is a choice, and it's easy.

But a choice to do what, exactly?

What the universe sent my way next took me by surprise.

*

SEVEN

GASPAR

"The future influences the present."
Friedrich Nietzsche

He caught my eye as he stocked bags of potato chips on the shelf. My coworker and I had to make a quick stop at the local convenience store while on our break at work to replenish our cigarettes.

"How are you, Gaspar?" She asked.

"Awesome. How are you?"

Gaspar and my friend had a brief, friendly conversation. She invited him to join us on our smoke break to which he politely declined and we continued out the door for our regularly scheduled lung destruction. As soon as we got outside the building, I couldn't help myself. I wanted to know *everything*.

"OMG, WHO IS HE?"

She explained that he was hired a few weeks ago and she really hadn't talked to him too much but she'd drop in a good word the next time she ran into him.

Before long, it was again time for me to purchase a new box of ciggies. My coworker called out sick this particular morning so I wandered down to the store solo to grab my refill and crossed my fingers that he would be there… And sure enough, he was.

"Hey! You're Laura, right?"

My stomach did a backflip. *He knew my name?!* My friend obviously already talked to him.

"Hi, yeah! How are you?"

To my surprise, actual words came out of my mouth; I was expecting gibberish and miscellaneous noises. We spoke for a few moments before he asked me for my number, and thus began one of the sweetest relationships I was ever a part of. Shortly after, we arranged our first date. To say I was overjoyed would be a considerable understatement.

The day of our date arrived and I anxiously awaited the moment I could escape my desk. When the hands on the clock struck six, he met me outside my building and we embarked on an evening of innocent fun together. We played billiards and split a pitcher of cheap beer. We laughed and shared stories and teased each other when we missed a shot. Neither one of us was able to stop smiling. We lost track of time, and when we realized how late it was getting, we closed our tab and headed outside.

The butterfly feeling had returned to my stomach and it was here to stay… for a couple months, at least. He walked me to my car, opened my door and gave me a kiss on the cheek.

Sigh.

Like *seriously*? This guy was a gentleman, too?! Just like that, my faith in dating was restored. I was all in. Gaspar was the one I was waiting for. We continued to spend time together at any and every opportunity we could until one day, he offered to make me dinner and I graciously accepted the invitation. I'd be crazy not to!

When I arrived, Gaspar crafted a beautiful pizza (from scratch). My developing female brain established this guy was boyfriend material. While we were cuddling and drifting off to sleep, he whispered something about love in my ear *in Spanish.* I, of course, played dumb and pretended I had no idea what he said, though it was perhaps one of the most wonderful things anyone ever murmured there. (Note: I don't speak Spanish, but I recognize words.) We were both in love (lust) with each other already. *That was fast*, I thought. I'm pretty positive it had only been about three weeks since we first met, but I have a need for speed and the driving record to prove it. That was the best date to date. I forgot about all my exes. I forgot about Dawson. I forgot about everyone. Gaspar was my clean slate.

The alarm went off relatively early. We put on our clothes and went outside to the patio to enjoy a cigarette together. The sun was shining bright, the temperature was pleasant and the day was young. Gaspar stared into my eyes and I looked up into his. His pupils were dilating like he was intoxicated, and I'm pretty positive mine were behaving the same way. I felt like I was looking directly into his soul and he into mine.

"Do you want to be my girlfriend?" He asked.

"I would love to." I smiled.

THIS was what I was looking for from the start.

He kissed me. Dopamine ran through my veins like an electric current. I certainly didn't expect that question on this fabulous morning but I was dreaming about our future together all night long. Later that same morning, we ran into his parents. We literally went from zero to a hundred overnight.

As you might imagine, we sprinted through the honeymoon phase equally as fast.

***

About a month later, we accomplished "comfortable," the mindset of believing no further energy is necessary in order to maintain the current situation. It started when we went on a group date where both he and his friend "forgot their wallets," leaving me and the other guy's girlfriend to pay the tab. He was staying over almost every night and neglecting to clean up after himself nor contributing in any other way. I felt like I was supporting him, though I was doing this exact thing to Ben years prior without realizing it. In the same way that he was depending on me for financial support, I was depending on him for emotional support. It is not acceptable to be dependent on anyone other than ourselves for anything. Period.

I was working and going to school full-time simultaneously, and though I wanted him to be there for me when I needed him, I also wanted him to respect my space. I never told him what was going on in my life or how I was feeling no matter how many times he asked.

One morning he took a shower at my apartment and left his clothes and wet towel on the floor of my bathroom. That was the straw that broke my back, I couldn't deal with it. There were no boundaries. I had to reclaim my personal space because I gave it all away.

We made plans "to talk."

He was avoiding me like the plague. It was a deeply emotional conversation because we both genuinely cared for each other yet knew this wasn't working for either of us. By the end of the conversation, we were both balling our eyes out. We reached a fork in the road and decided to go different directions. It was mutual.

Again, I was exiled to loneliness in the kingdom of singledom, a place that was still so very foreign to me as a serial monogamist. I didn't know it yet, but the difference was that this time, it was for good.

LESSON #7
Codependency is unhealthy.

I was attracting and dating people who had not figured out who they were yet and I was unable to comprehend that because I was in no way a fully matured adult myself. We are attracted to people that give off the same type of energy that we do or are envious of. We were far too young to consider a future together because we were too dazed and confused to see our individual futures. We were depending on each other for what we thought we needed *at the time*.

We had a relationship complete with all stages of a longer one compacted into the span of a few months. We were strangers who found interest each other, shared our lives with each other, got to know each other's friends, and then changed our minds. We were all in, then all out. Where did he see himself in ten years? Where was I going to be? How many kids did he want? Where did he want to live the rest of his life? Gaspar and I were holding the temporary position of boyfriend/girlfriend in each other's lives, but for what? What mutual goal were we heading towards?

I didn't have the courage to define my boundaries with my living situation or money. I wanted to have someone beside me at night because I didn't want to be alone, so I gave him whatever he needed to stay until I couldn't do it anymore. We loved each other in an unhealthy way.

Our relationship happened so fast, we were practically still strangers when we committed to each other. I vowed to myself that I wouldn't commit to anyone else unless I knew I could do so forever, and to this day I remain single.

After my realization that I should not go around hanging out or hooking up with anyone else from home after Felix, it was time for me to jump on the train with the rest of the millennial generation and start looking for my future husband using a more unconventional method—

Swiping.

*

Part II
Ruthless Dating

EIGHT

HAROLD

*"Advertising is the art of convincing people to spend money
they don't have for something they don't need."*
Will Rogers

My sister wouldn't stop raving about this new dating app thing she was playing. She made it sound like online shopping, but for boys, and I was intrigued. I was never particularly fond of shopping for clothes (or anything, for that matter) because I hate spending money on nonsense I don't need, but an app for finding a boyfriend? This was something I could get behind... to find someone that would get behind me.

Online dating always looked like a joke; there was this stereotype and negative connotation attached and I did not want to be associated with it. People do not like things they do not understand, so it was inevitable that online dating would initially get a bad reputation. No one yet understood it in 2013. For whatever reason, back then, I thought people on the apps were desperate, and maybe they are sometimes, but I never wanted to be perceived that way. On the other hand, there were thousands of boys who created profiles to advertise their "best" selves just waiting to be matched with. I wanted to know what else was out there; this was the opportunity I was waiting for. If I wasn't exploring all the options available, what was I doing? (Not a brilliant mindset, by the way. It is important to remain selective in our choices!) My previous dating experiences gave me the insight I thought I needed to find my future husband out in the wild, but holy hell, I was not ready to surf the wave headed towards me at all.

It was exciting to cast a line into the ocean and see what types of fish were out there. Was my "soulmate" waiting for me online? Advertisements and blogs were enough to convince me that tons of people were doing it. Dating apps were full of possibilities, but the success rate still seemed to reflect that of the millennial IRL... incredibly rare (at the time, most people I knew were also single). What did I have to lose? As Blink-182 once said, "Nobody likes you when you're twenty-three," so I had pretty low expectations for myself that year. It seemed like there were only gains to be had. Unless we get out there and take risks, we will never know for sure.

I downloaded the app. The question now was, who did I want to be? How is my profile going to depict that?

For days I stressed about the details. I created something that would portray the fun and flirty version of myself using a sequence of basic Emojis and a few photos that were outdated; I'd give it an "**F**" knowing what I know now. I only had about a dozen quality pictures of myself from the recent past to choose from since most of the photos I had also included my exes or I was wasted, or they were *so* old it would just be inappropriate to use on an adult dating site. I wonder how long it would take to get banned? It happened once to me already on Xbox—my gamertag was "partyinmypantys" before someone flagged it for being inappropriate. For my dating profile I was not going to go in the sexual direction, though, so I followed all the vanilla dating advice provided by the Internet; drowning my personality out to reflect that of what is now commonly known as "basic."

We love "basic" because it is common and therefore, easy; it is what the majority of others have agreed is good. Basic requires no thought. Basic is the status quo. The more basic we are, the less we are our selves. Why are we so focused on what everyone else is doing? With that said, my "basic" profile should give you a pretty good indication as to what the first round of men I matched with were like, so let's briefly talk about a couple of those who shaped the way I used the apps, beginning with Harold, *my first ever* online date following the summer in which I moved to Los Angeles.

***

I sat on my patio for hours every night getting stoned and staring at photos of all the eligible men within a ten-mile radius. There were so many! Swiping through boys was more fun than I ever imagined it would be; in fact, it was highly addictive. It seemed as though there was an endless supply of profiles to review, and the number of matches skyrocketed after my first few days of online presence. There are few things in this universe that provide a greater ego boost than the one of knowing people think you are attractive. Eventually it got to my head.

Apps were a very new phenomenon and thus, there really wasn't much advice for me to base decisions from. I had no alternative other than to rely on my own trials and errors. Millennials are the Guinea pigs of this new, hybrid tech-dating age— we are the last generation known to mankind to be born before widespread Internet usage and cell phones, both of these now seem to be a requirement of functioning in modern society.

He's pretty cute, I thought. The profile was as white-bread as mine. It was comprised of four photos; two of which were visibly outdated. The bio section was bland; it listed his height and a couple of Emojis. Who am I to judge? Mine was equally lacking. Because it was my first attempt at online dating, I had no clue how to advertise myself to the audience I was trying to attract, primarily because I didn't know exactly who that audience was. For the time being, I was focused on physical appearance, but I never considered myself to have a type. The people I dated in Part I all looked nothing like each other.

I swiped Harold to the right. It was a match!

The details of our initial conversation are a blur to me now, but it was *hilarious*. He struck me as a kinda fratty, football jock type powered by a few too many energy drinks. We exchanged numbers and migrated our banter outside the app.

We made plans to meet for coffee the following day after work at a little place in my hood. I arrived at the café and about ten minutes past our scheduled time, my phone buzzed.

Sorry, I'm on my way over there now. Got stuck at work.

On his way?

I was frustrated, but I understood. I was steadily late to things in my life and I wanted to give him the benefit of the doubt— maybe he didn't realize what time it was. What if the boss put something on his plate right before he walked out the door? It happens. It could be *anything*. Work was my number one priority, so I assumed it was his as well. And everyone else's.

I waited... and waited, then waited some more. I am no stranger to waiting, just as you probably aren't. My whole life, I felt like I've been waiting. Not just in terms of waiting for my "soulmate," though—I'm talking about waiting for *everything*— Waiting in line, waiting for test scores to be posted, waiting for my mother to pick me up after school or my dad to get home from work, waiting for better days, waiting for a vacation, waiting for the clock to hit a specific hour, waiting for a sign, waiting to fall asleep at night or waiting for an apology.

Waiting is a waste of time unless you are able to make the best use of it in between the current moment and that moment you are waiting for. The entire point of time is now. If your head is in the past or future, it's not here.

So as I sipped my way through my first couple cups of coffee, I planned the rest of my evening and did some researching for other creative projects I was working on. I may have done some scrolling through social media or Pinterest in between. I'm a pro at waiting.

It's a good thing it takes a lot to scare me off because most people would probably not use an online dating app to meet another person if this was their first experience, but not me. It looked like he was standing me up, but I knew he wasn't. I was determined and desperate to find my "soulmate" no matter what I had to do or what I had to go through. What if Harold and I just had to meet in person to know?

Ten minutes later, I looked down at my phone to see a message from him saying he was a few lights away. By this point he was already half an hour late, but I continued to wait patiently outside on the patio in the crisp evening breeze as I watched the sun sink below the skyline.

Cafés always felt like home to me. This was no exception.

Almost forty-five minutes after the time we agreed to meet, Harold graced me with his presence. He apologized for his delay, blamed it on work and the traffic and greeted each other with a hug. Heavily caffeinated, I accompanied him to the counter and he ordered the largest sugary drink they had to offer. I requested another refill for my coffee and made my way to the condiment bar to add the good stuff.

He wanted to sit inside so we found a corner and started learning about each other. We had a few things in common—he was a nerd and he smoked weed—two things that often seem to be connected with each other. He told me about his fraternity status in college, his sports accomplishments, his degree, and his friends. By the end of our conversation, I felt he was a good guy on paper.

I extended an invitation for him to join me in smoking a bowl, so we walked down the street to my apartment. Now, it might seem like common sense—don't invite strangers into your home (duh)—but not for me. Allow me to remind you that I've always been the type of person who lives dangerously, and for the majority of my childhood I had more platonic male friendships than healthy female ones. My roommates were both present, what was the worst that could happen?

Harold and I walked outside to my balcony. The ledge was draped in a twisted line of purple and orange lights and vibrant furniture complete with an unnecessary number of accent pillows (as most female homes do). My roomies and I were obsessed with candles so they lined almost every flat surface we had. It was the perfect place to fall in love.

We continued chatting about whatever it was that we were talking about at the coffee shop while I packed a healthy bowl of greens for us to share and handed him the bong. He struck the lighter and took an incredibly long, slow inhale before hacking up one of his lungs. He didn't smoke as much as he claimed he did.

"Oh, that's pretty good weed," he muttered in between coughs.

"It's medical." I informed him. When it came to marijuana, I was able to out-smoke just about anyone. I was always high, 24/7 for about a decade; this was just the beginning. To say I had a problem would be a major understatement; I was incredible at pretending like it wasn't.

Harold and I began streaming an episode of something on TV while my roomie worked on her homework assignment at the computer. Not even ten minutes passed before Harold and I started making out. Meanwhile, my roommate continued to mind her own business on the other side of the room with an oversized pair of headphones covering her ears which I can only hope blocked out the sounds of our lips smacking against each other.

"Can you kick your roommate out of here so we can have some privacy?"

Woah. That came out of nowhere. I was shocked.

He wanted to have sex (something I was not interested in doing right now). However, this was his assumption by my inviting him over to my place to begin with; and now we were making out. There was no good reason for me to bring him there, I was trying to bond with him by engaging in one of our shared interests—smoking weed, *not* having sex. But here we were.

It was getting late and I suggested we go outside and smoke one final bowl. He tried to convince me to get rid of my roommate, and again I refused. We passed the bong back and forth a few times and he literally stood up, opened the door and walked out. No "see you later," no "thank you," no *nothing*. To this day, I have yet to encounter anyone quite like him.

My New Year's Resolution in my early twenties was always to make better bad decisions; and to me, all of this was a brilliant bad idea. I was wrong; it was just a bad idea. He taught me the importance of really filtering through dating profiles.

LESSON #8
Judge people by the amount of <u>effort</u> they put in.

First impressions say a lot more about someone than we think. Profile photos are simply the bait that hooks us (or not). It doesn't matter how good looking a person is; if a profile is lacking personality, then the person on the other side of the device probably is, too. A dating profile reflects how much effort an individual is willing to put into you. If a dating profile looks incomplete, chances are, that person probably isn't going to add value to your life.

No person should invest energy in pursuing someone who isn't spending their time and energy on the quality of their own profile. This is the easiest way to determine who is undeserving of our own time so we can filter them out without having to feel as though we are missing out because we're not. People with low-effort profiles aren't looking for anything serious, they're looking for something to chase and as soon as they catch it or discover they cannot, they will chase something else. This trend is true throughout many aspects of life, not just in dating.

Dating profiles are advertisements. Don't be duped by the photos, *always* read the fine print *and* ask a lot of questions. If the advertisement doesn't get your attention, neither would the product on a shelf in real life. If someone doesn't put any effort into them self, do you really think they're going to put any effort into you? Maybe meeting strangers from the internet was going to be more difficult than I thought. Maybe the only thing guys wanted to find was sex, after all. That's what I was brainwashed to believe.

But another part of me understood that men wanted a lot more than sex. We wanted the same thing—growing up with mostly male friends gave me the insight I needed to understand that much. Guys were always my friends before sex was added to the mix.

After my first online date, I was able to move forward knowing that it was safe as long as you meet people in public and *not* at your house, though I did this a few more times before officially coming to that conclusion. Then in a sea full of strangers, I managed to find a familiar fish.

*

NINE

IVAN

"The cost of a thing is the amount of what I call life which is required to be exchanged for it, immediately or in the long run."
Henry David Thoreau

What if my "soulmate" walked up and down the same halls as me but it was never our destiny to connect with each other until right now, here on the internet? I don't recall any conversations growing up, but heck, why not start now? I briefly entertained the idea before responding to his captivating opening line that landed in my inbox, which read a little something like this:

Hey! We went to the same school!

I know, right? Dreamy. His message didn't need to be creative or clever or anything, for that matter because I was already interested. Since we both knew of each other, we were able to rule out catfish rubbish (though that never once stopped me, nor was I ever catfished in my extensive history of online dates). Ivan and I both knew with 100% certainty that the other person was, in fact, a real person. We would unquestionably have some things (and people) to talk about. We immediately exchanged contact info and set up a time and place for drinks.

My sequence of missteps commenced the moment I agreed to meet him at his apartment. I reckoned this would be harmless because I knew him. He explained there was free parking on his street and the bar was only a couple blocks away, so the plan would be to walk over there once I parked. It made perfect sense.

The breeze was cool and sun was starting to set when I pulled up. I parked my car and rang Ivan as I walked in the direction of his building. I was looking forward to getting to know this familiar face in an unfamiliar place. He met me at sidewalk level and we set towards our destination on foot.

This particular bar was my kind of bar. There were so many beers on tap, I hadn't a clue where to start. Thankfully, Ivan did; this *was* his local watering hole after all. We covered the basics and what we'd been up to since graduation. We both loved to travel and drink beer so there was no shortage of topics to discuss nor stories to tell.

Ivan asked the bartender for beer recommendations so I sat back and listened while the two talked hops. A great deal of deliberation later, an impeccably poured glass of a tasty lager was placed in front of me with a beautiful head of foam perched on top. After that one, there was another. And another. Then, maybe another? I'm not totally sure—no one was keeping track, not even the bartender (according to the tab) and the more I had, the less I counted. Ivan just kept asking for another round and the next thing I knew, we were both plastered. Each time a fresh beer was placed in front of me, I simply would not allow it to go to waste. Consuming every last drop was my responsibility and duty to alcoholics worldwide; it was in honor of those who continued to practice these traditions during the dark days of prohibition.

Ivan kept bringing up a video he and some of his friends made while they were travelling abroad after graduation. It sounded interesting, I enjoy travel as well and figured I could watch it before dipping out since my car was parked outside his place anyways. I could feel that he was getting a bit touchy, and I knew it was a bad idea, but I agreed to go into his apartment anyways. With all the alcohol running through my veins, I was empowering the instinctual part of me that wanted to have sex. I was way too drunk to drive, so regardless of whatever happened that night, I'm glad I accepted his invitation.

He waved to the bartender for our check and before I could grab my wallet out of my purse, Ivan covered *the whole tab*. I felt grateful that he wanted to pay for my drinks. My body was overflowing with warm, fuzzy feelings.

When we got back to his place, he immediately rushed over to the TV to start the video he wouldn't stop babbling about at the bar, and it was only seconds after we sat down that he moved in on my face. He was confident that after getting me in his apartment, he'd be getting in me tonight, and that's definitely what it looked like; I was hammered. I did not see sex in our deck of cards, so why was I leading him to believe it might be?

Things started getting hot and heavy and we did stuff, but thankfully in the exact moment my underwear was in danger of separating from my body, my phone started going off. I snapped out of it and jumped off his bed. The timing literally could not have been better—talk about divine intervention!

"Hey, I have to go. My roommate locked herself out of our apartment and I need to get back to let her in. It's getting late anyways..." I knew I needed to get out of there ASAP.

"Oh, please stay just a little longer! The video is almost over." A little bit longer is all anyone needs to make something happen. *Just a little bit longer* is the "just one cigarette" of sex. He tried pulling me back on top of him and I resisted, so he insisted on walking me to my car. We went outside and shared an empty kiss before I felt his lips pull away from mine and then, he dropped the bomb.

"I forgot my keys... I can't get back into my apartment."

"Maybe your roommate can let you in...?" Unfortunately, he *also* left his phone inside, and was therefore unable to contact him. I handed Ivan my phone so he could attempt but in today's world, a lack of your cell phone also means a lack of contact information because people don't memorize phone numbers anymore. Nowadays we have infinite other bits of useless information we want to store in our craniums and phone numbers don't make the cut because we have phones for that. I suggested that he log into his social media and connect with a friend or family member there.

His luck was diminishing faster than my patience as it was closing in on midnight. Eventually he just started surfing his feed, and I knew I needed to get out of there. He was running out of options and started bouncing some new ideas off me. Though I do have an appreciation for creative solutions, it was in this moment that his requests took a turn for the ridiculous.

"What if I came home with you and stayed the night at your house, then you drove me back in the morning?"

"I can't, I have work early in the morning..."

"What if we stay together in a hotel room down the street and I pay you back tomorrow?"

"No, I'm sorry, I have to get home..."

"What if we both slept here in your car?"

This guy would not give up!

My phone started ringing. Ivan's father was returning his call, but there was nothing he could do that would make any difference to resolve the current predicament. Midnight had come and gone. Exhaustion was looming heavily over me, and I was out of patience.

"I'm really sorry, I have to leave. I have to be up so I can get ready for work in a few hours and my roommate still needs me to let her in."

"Fine."

He got out of my car and told me he'd sit in the garage by his roommate's parking spot until he got home.

I pulled away from the curb with my rap music blaring and sped off into the night, windows rolled down and a freshly lit cigarette resting between my fingers. I was exhausted, frustrated and still fairly intoxicated. Before I even reached the freeway, my phone went off, which, of course, was Ivan. His roommate arrived sheer moments after I left him outside. I was not interested in having sex with him and thus, should not have entered his apartment, but because I drank too much, I trailed him in there.

LESSON #9
Everything costs something.

There is a price, or an opportunity cost, for everything in life and it doesn't necessarily mean money is involved. We are accustomed to thinking this way because of the capitalist society we exist in, and we attribute an extreme amount of our attention and worth to monetary value above almost all else, but if we dive deeper, we are paying a lot more for things than we realize. For a moment, I'm going to put you in the mind of a business person—

Q: What is the cost of you reading this book?

A: Whatever you paid or didn't pay for it plus the amount of time it takes you to read it, and all of the other things you might be able to do with that time.

Wanna try another one?

Q: What does a shot at the bar cost?

A: Alcohol costs a few bucks in addition to your sobriety and your ability to make good decisions. It will probably also cost you another shot, and so on... The more shots, the more hours of tomorrow you spend in your bed.

Think you're getting the hang of this?

Q: What does the #2 with a large drink and fries cost you?

A: Junk food costs you a few bucks plus the amount of time and discomfort it takes you to expel it in the bathroom later, plus the potential need to use more money to purchase clothes that fit you better later if it becomes a habit. And just in case you wanted to try and eat something healthy to get nutrients, you realize you don't even want it because there's no room in your stomach for that now.

Q: What does a shopping habit cost you?

A: Your hard-earned money, and more of your time and eventually storage space unless you can learn to let things go, otherwise you'll always need more and more space. The more stuff you have, the more time you spend trying to figure out what to do with it, where to put it or how to get rid of it.

Q: What is the cost of a chance?
A: Only a gambler knows because a gambler chooses his bid, but like any addiction, it can cost you everything.

Q: What was the cost of going out with Ivan?
A: It cost us both a few hours of sobriety, we were wasted. I almost gave him everything I had to offer until the moment my phone went off and snapped me out of my drunken state. Getting as drunk as I did also cost me my best the following day at work since I was tired and hungover, as I'm sure he was as well if he went. Our collective behavior resulted in the decision for neither of us to be interested in seeing the other again. We might of exchanged a couple more messages before falling off the face of our phones.

Why did I drink that much with Ivan? I was too weak to decline the beer he continued to place in front of me because my alcohol addiction was the most out of control addiction I had. Getting drunk made me feel cool. (Fun fact: getting totally trashed isn't cool, it's dumb.) The more I had to drink, the harder saying "no" became. I got so drunk I failed to set any boundaries. Every decision we make costs something—we either have the choice to pay our own price or pay what someone or something else is asking for. We have both the choice and authority to choose.

Someone who keeps offering to buy you more drinks is trying to get you drunk. Alcohol makes anyone easier to sway. *The person who uses alcohol to aid in their attempt to get something from you insists on getting you another drink before you have finished the one already sitting in front of you.* If you can't or wouldn't say "no" to another drink, what else wouldn't you say "no" to? Those who do not have pure intentions will try to find out.

An investor only invests in what they believe will provide a return, and there's always risk that it's not going to pay out. In the business world, for example (I'm not talking about *Happy Hour* with a few coworkers), it is not unheard of for an executive or person of authority to drink with potential business partners or clients prior to closing or negotiating a deal. It is a means of getting to know someone on a personal level, and when we feel personally connected to others, we are more heavily influenced by them. Alcohol is a huge aid for this.

People don't generally just try to get you drunk because you're cuter or funnier that way, it makes the process of getting something from you easier because you are less self-aware and less capable of rational decision making.

Addictive behavior is predictable behavior, thus incredibly easy to take advantage of because when an addict gets something they think they "need," they want more of it as to maintain the temporary feeling of gratification it provides them with. A drunk person does not make the same decisions a sober person does. I never intended on having sex with Ivan that night and thankfully he was respectful enough as to not force it as Dawson had. I was never the kind of girl who slept with someone on the first date, but here I was doing (almost) exactly that.

*

TEN

JARED

"A clear rejection is always better than a fake promise."
Zig Ziglar

I'll keep this one short because what I think we should all take away from this experience is one thing: Who pays the bill?

This age old question has been answered a million times, but why does it matter? The answer is in the intentions of the two people who have the bill in front of them.

***

Jared was undoubtedly wittier, wealthier and wiser than many men I met on the internet. His profile was thorough and included reviews from "real women," some of which he dated, some were friends, and one even came from his mother. He had an *over*-abundance of effort in his profile; the exact opposite of Harold. We had similar interests and according to the dating site, nearly perfect compatibility. By this point, I'd completely revamped my dating profile. It was now *also* burdened with an excessive amount of effort; it definitely made sense why we matched. He was adventurous, hard-working and curious. His salt and pepper hair signaled maturity and he said he was looking for "The One." I wanted that, too.

My lady-brain went off on millions of tangents of all the ways our futures might play out. I imagined him being a fantastic father to our children. He was quite a few years older; his life experience was unmatched by anyone I met and far exceeded my own. We were on different levels from the start.

Our virtual conversation was fluid and intriguing and I was excited to continue it in real life. When the evening of our date arrived, we sat down in a booth across from each other. Words of physics, mathematics, and biology trickled from our mouths. Boring to you, maybe, but this is the kind of stuff I think about in my free time. These are the intangible tools our species created as a language for understanding, explaining, and predicting the world around us. I wanted to know more about him and what made him think the way he did since we apparently thought a lot alike. Would he be the variable that solved my equation?

Often, we encounter awkward silences on dates, but with Jared, they felt painfully long. Neither one of us could think of personal questions to ask. Maybe we weren't as compatible with each other as our match percentage led us to believe? Maybe we were *too* alike? Were we both out of touch with our emotions, or was it only me? Connection was missing. After the second round of drinks, it appeared we both made up our mind about our future— there wasn't one.

This was not personal and we both knew it. Early stages of dating are all about picking up hints and reading people from a combination of what they do, what they say, *and* what they don't. This is where that whole "who pays the bill" shenanigans comes into play. I firmly believe that we are all responsible for ourselves; that goes for all occasions from dinner with friends or acquaintances, to an unexpected dinner, or even lunch with a boss. Online "dates" (or any date for that matter) are no exception.

When the bill comes, I <u>always</u> grab my wallet. Period.

Many women argue that because women put in a lot of time, money and effort to get dressed up for dates, men *should* pay. I definitely understand why many women see it this way as it can and often does take a lot of time and effort to appeal to beauty standards, but we don't HAVE to do any of that stuff. We don't HAVE to buy a new outfit when we have a first date. We don't HAVE to cake our face with half an inch of powder and cream. Why do we feel like we do? Are we really that insecure in our own skin? Regardless, believing that men should pay <u>because</u> we spend our time and money on these things is the type of absurd thinking that gets us in trouble. This is the mindset of keeping score, which is toxic in itself. In my experience, men want to pay if they want to see you again.

Jared did *not* offer to pay for my drinks so we split the bill, and because I already had my wallet out there was no awkward requirement to have a conversation about it. When it comes down to it, we should all be focusing on getting to know the person we are in the presence of, not who is supposed to pay.

In keeping my promise in that this one is short—

<u>LESSON #10</u>
Not everything must be said out loud to be heard clearly.

However, some things do because we cannot read people's minds or expect them to read ours. Say goodbye to awkward bill moments. If we started observing behavior, we would all understand each other better. It's time to end this debate for good.

1. Expect to pay for yourself. When the bill arrives, reach for your wallet like you normally would if you were out with a friend. Why are you assuming this person is going to pay for you? Why do you want them to?
2. IF the other person *insists* on covering your bill, you have two options:
   a. Let them pay – this says "I'm interested" back. However, it can also mean a lot of other things, like "I'm just hanging out with you for free stuff," or "I'm not going to argue with you if you want to pay, so fine." Consider your intentions before accepting. ALWAYS say thank you. Expressing gratitude for generosity goes a long way.
   b. Pay for yourself – this can say a lot of things ranging from "I'm not that into you" to "I don't need/want that" to "I don't know yet," or "I'm not ready to consider this a date." If they insist and you still don't want to allow it, simply insist that you are paying for yourself.
3. Stop caring about who pays, because it doesn't matter. If you don't have any money or don't want to think about it, go on dates where there's no bill—like a hike or picnic or something outdoors, there are plenty of free activities out there. Be creative; I know you have it in you.

If a person doesn't offer to pay for you, it does not mean they are not interested. No one owes you anything. You are the only person experiencing what the other person's intentions are.

As you can see, it's simple, and if it's complicated, you probably shouldn't be out with them. "Who pays the bill?" is a hot topic; but it doesn't matter who pays the damn bill. The whole thing is just a ridiculous debate that makes men look like jerks for not paying and women look entitled for wanting them to. Men should never feel obligated to pay for women just like women should never assume men are going to pay for them. Paying the bill is intended to be a nice gesture and nothing else. Women hooking up with men who take them on fancy dates is basically just an evolved form of prostitution.

The purpose of dating is to get to know the person you are on the date with, not worry about what happens when the bill shows up. If things are meant to be, they will be, and the bill will probably have nothing to do with it. How your date treats you and the wait staff is far more important than who's paying. If you're going to pay attention to anything, that's far more telling about someone's character. Jared and I were a near perfect match on paper, but numeric values don't always correlate to the real world.

Each case is unique.

Jared was the first guy that split the bill with me on the first date. Nothing grew between us that night or any night that followed. Rejection happens. No one is everyone's cup of tea, *that's life*. To be universally liked would be boring anyways. I don't know what that's from, but someone more important than me said it once upon a time (I can't find the quote).

*

ELEVEN

KURT

"Monsters are real, and ghosts are real too.
They live inside us, and sometimes, they win."
Stephen King

In the raw version of this journaling (before I converted it into what it is now), this chapter did not exist. I skipped over it like it never happened because I was not triggered on the topic until I later began editing it. There are a lot of things I would do differently if in this situation again thanks to what I now know about mental health.

***

My online experience was loaded with unexpected moments, but I wanted to slow down and fall into something more serious since the holidays were coming up. For the first time in my dating life, I was single and not ready to face them alone. One cloudy morning, Kurt's message sat at the top of my inbox. It was a lengthy paragraph loaded with sweet nothings and silly puns. I smiled after I read it. It was a lovely break from the ordinary "Hey," the corny pick-up lines, and the spam requests for sex that typically flooded in.

He promised me the moon. Literally.

I wanted to know more. Even his literary skills were on point.

We sent paragraphs to each other for a few days before making plans to meet in real life. We had so much in common, from our interests and hobbies to the loads of individual issues we were dealing with—the difference was that he was getting help to fix his. I still didn't realize I had any.

For our first date, Kurt took me to his favorite local Italian spot. We chatted for far longer than I expected we would. After dinner we grabbed frozen yogurt from the place next door and sat down on a bench to eat it. He walked me to my car and gave me a kiss on the cheek. I went home that night elated.

Every day we were texting or talking on the phone. Our conversations were effortless. Being with Kurt was a completely new experience because it forced me to remember how to be sober since I rarely ever was. He didn't drink and I'd never online-dated anyone without drinking alcohol on the dates before.

We once went to a baseball game and I accompanied him in his sobriety. I had a blast; in fact, I had more fun at that game than I had at some others in which I *was* drinking. I was beginning to think about sleeping with him but he never made a move and I was never the type to initiate it. I still understood the immense value of sex in my sobriety even though I already slept with quite a few people.

> *Hey! My roommate is having a party tonight.*
> *Want to come keep me company?*

He promised we could still play beer pong even though we wouldn't be drinking and as soon as things turned up he planned to start up the karaoke machine. Refraining from drinking or smoking at a party was a bizarre experience, but I learned a lot about both myself and him that night.

When it was time for me to leave, he walked me out to my car and we stayed outside for a bit to talk in the cool evening breeze. He opened up about some heavy matters to me that I never discussed with anyone before. He was a recovering substance abuse addict and had attempted suicide several times. The drug part I anticipated given the sobriety stuff, but the suicide part terrified me. I didn't understand mental illness at the time. Why would he want to take his own life?

I drove home unable to stop thinking about what he divulged to me. Not only was I already fearful of love, but now I was thinking about how unstable it would be with him. At any given moment, he might decide this life isn't worth it anymore and choose to disappear into another one. Instead of supporting him and thanking him for being so open and honest with me, I ran straight back to my own substance abuse. I distanced myself. I had feelings for him, but things were getting too serious and I was terrified. I knew I would be a terrible influence on him with my own horrific drinking and smoking patterns, which I managed to completely hide from him. I was emotionally dead.

I faded from *his* life like a ghost. Like he wasn't even human.

LESSON #11
Ghosting is the result of being dead to one's self.

There are a lot of different reasons it happens, but no one deserves to be ghosted. It is the result of choosing to ignore our own monsters; it has nothing to do with the other person. People who exhibit ghostly behavior have a lot of inner work to complete before they are capable of loving someone else in a healthy way, so if you are ghosted, consider yourself lucky. We can ask a ghost for a reason, but still we may never receive a response. Ghosting is a direct reflection of what is going on within the person doing the ghosting.

I ghosted people because I thought it was normal. It happened to me so many times that I just considered it to be a normal part of dating, I didn't realize the damage I was inflicting on others. Being ghosted made me feel alone, abandoned, ignored, and worthless. I didn't want to be honest with Kurt because I was afraid of hurting him. Kurt trusted me with some of his most dreadful monsters and I thought it would be best if I just disappeared because I didn't know how to battle them either.

Kurt made three or four sincere attempts to reconnect with me before he gave up. One of his final messages called me out on ghosting him. My behavior was coldhearted; not only was I unable to confront him about what I was feeling, I wasn't even able to confront myself. Here was a perfectly good guy; I said I wanted to be in love with someone but here was my opportunity and I couldn't do it.

We never spoke again...

Nor will we ever.

I was gone like the wind, ready to blow on someone new. Sex was a priority for me and I wasn't getting it from Kurt. I hadn't slept with anyone in months. I was yearning for physical connection because I didn't understand my "need" for sex.

I thought it would be better to start informing men I wasn't looking for anything serious before they got involved. If they were aware that I just wanted to have fun from the get-go, at least that would be a warning. After Kurt, I was ghosting people regularly, drinking with men I had no interest in seeing again, sleeping around, and living an insanely hollow and dangerous lifestyle. I was chasing empty highs and hiding as much as I could from my friends and family.

I'll never be able to apologize—I found out about a year later he chose to stop fighting his monsters. People commit suicide for many different reasons and I'll never know what his was. All I know is that people who make the attempt are so unhappy in this reality, the thought of not feeling anything ever again is actually better than facing the continued pain of theirs. I'd be lying if I alleged it never crossed my mind, but I always resorted to other means of self-harm (drugs). Suicide and all other forms of self-harm are the complete absence of self-love.

For a long time, I blamed myself for having something to do with Kurt's departure from this universe. He grew close enough to me to tell me about his dark past and I didn't know what I was supposed to do since I didn't understand emotions at all, I couldn't even figure out my own. I must accept that it was his decision but it made me realize I really needed to stop ghosting people. I had somehow rationalized the behavior as "acceptable." I never wanted to hurt him nor did I owe him an explanation, but the least I could have done was be a friend because that's what you do when you care about someone. I cared about Kurt. I care about all the people in my life—past, present, and future.

There are better ways to end relationships than to ignore someone. You can literally type this into Google, "things to say instead of ghosting." Nothing is more valuable than the truth, even when it's difficult, vague, or ugly; just keep it light, positive, and constructive. Until I'm able to communicate with actual ghosts, I'll never be able to apologize. The least I could've done was treat him with enough respect to be honest with him.

For the love of love, please don't ghost any loving, breathing humans you meet in life. Honesty doesn't have to be complicated and a little goes a long way. If you're not feeling something, just say so, it's not them, it's you. And that's okay. But say it, because you may later realize how messed up it was and never get the chance to apologize. The first time I was ghosted by someone, I thought it was because there was something wrong with me. I now realize it was *their* issue and that it had nothing to do with me, but it sure felt like it did. Not caring about other's feelings and time isn't cool. Does a person behave this way because they don't value their own feelings?

***

On another note, Halloween was just around the corner.

I was pumped and already playing the part. Though I was ashamed, to take my mind off the fact I just ghosted someone for no good reason I decided I would look for someone who made me feel better about myself; someone else who was dead inside, too, or dead enough at least.

Someone who was just as horny as I was.

*

TWELVE

LYLE

"Sex without love is as hollow and ridiculous as love without sex."
Hunter S. Thomson

"Single" was proving to be more lonely than I was able to cope with. I was blindly progressing down a dark tunnel that would grow much, much darker; *wayyy* more than fifty shades. I ran off to find someone who *only* wanted sex. What if someone could meet just physical needs without emotional attachment?

A new mindset was brewing in my lady-brain.

The more people I dated, the more I wondered if I was ever going to be *satisfied* with just one person, or if I would be enough to *satisfy* any one of them either. There were thousands of men out there but it was uncommon anyone maintained my attention longer than one conversation because I was distracted so easily. I wanted to be able to have the amount of sex I was used to having from my previous relationships without drastically increasing my "number;" this was a safer alternative. My faith in monogamy was dwindling...

Hey sexy.

...He had me at *sex*.

No one *decides* to become an addict, it just happens.
Addicts are slaves to their bad habits. Like any other addict, the first one leads to another, and another, and another and then, BAM.

"Just one" turned into three-hundred-and-sixty-five. Addictions were never one single decision; they are a result of a repeated decision consistently rewarded by a good feeling or other form of positive reinforcement. That's why it becomes an addiction—there becomes not only a physical dependence, but also a *psychological* dependence, and THAT'S the part we fail to talk about. Addicts are on auto-pilot to say "yes" to the thing they are addicted to.

It happened and I didn't even see it.

This was the point my sex addiction started to run my life.

Up to this point, everyone I slept with (sober) was someone I "loved," at least in the sense that I interpreted the word. I believed love and sex to be one in the same, but was now beginning to consider that they were unrelated. Lyle supported this theory.

I was hoping to find someone strictly for satisfying carnal desires; so it would have to be an attractive man carrying plenty of red flags to discourage me from getting emotionally attached. Lyle was the first and only applicant need apply. Our mutual goal was to fulfill physical needs only. *Nothing else*. We legitimately had a full blown conversation about it before we even kissed each other to verbalize our understanding of the situation, and this is one of the primary reasons it lasted as long as it did. It felt just like a scene you would see in a movie.

I never intended on things progressing with Lyle; nor did he.

We were both 100% doing this for sex. 0% emotions.

"Meet me at my office. Let's see if we hit it off." I told him. I first wanted to meet him in a public place—I had to make sure he was the person I thought he was since that's the person I wanted to do the sex with.

Sure enough, Lyle was there at the drop of a hat. I liked that he was punctual, so he was off to a good start. I took my lunch break and we smoked a bowl in my car and chatted for almost an hour. I made him explain his current dating situation. I wanted to make sure we were on the same page. He stated that he was in an open relationship and was not interested in anything other than sex. It was a nearly perfect situation for both of us. We had nothing in common other than being attracted to each other and wanting only sex.

The new mindset I was in the process of adopting was to completely detach sex from emotions since I had a couple traumatic experiences when I was new to the scene. It seems to always be the case that when we become involved sexually with someone else; at least one person started with or develops feelings. Can two people sleep together without it resulting in an emotional attachment? *What if sex and emotions didn't have anything to do with each other? What if the human species was never designed to be monogamous and it actually was more instinctual for us to just have sex with whoever we wanted, whenever we wanted like the rest of the animals roaming the kingdom?*

It always appeared that men had it all figured out; Lyle was the absolute perfect person for me to learn from. He was not interested in romance, nor was I (with him) and we were very up front and honest about our intentions. This combination of things along with chemistry enabled our long-term success as two people having emotionless sex.

***

It started on Halloween.

We sent flirty texts to each other all day. The cock... I mean, the clock finally struck five-thirty and the festivities were underway, but before I went out to the bars, Lyle was going to stop by to help me take off the nerdy outfit I wore to work so I could change into something a little more inappropriate.

> *I'm outside.*

I darted out my front door to greet him at the curb and guide him upstairs to my apartment. We made our way to my balcony to share a bowl before the bang, and then, we did it. On his way out, he grabbed my head, fingers intertwined in my hair and pulled my face to his. We passionately kissed and he disappeared into the night. Our first night together was short but oh so sweet— we had the chemistry I longed for, and we were merely strangers. Thoughts about him raced through my mind and I struggled to make them stop. He was mysterious. I had no idea when I'd see him next, but I did know it would be soon.

What made my decision to have sex with Lyle different than any other guy was that for the first time, <u>I chose to use sex itself for the purpose of filling a void</u> instead of a way of genuinely connecting with someone. I chose to reprogram my mind as a coping mechanism rendering me incapable of realizing and finding the one and only thing I wanted. Therapy would have been a better option.

For *YEARS*, we met up for regular sessions on lunch breaks or in the later hours of the night until out of the blue, either he stopped hitting me up or I stopped responding to him because I was seeing someone I wanted to be exclusive with, something that only happened a few times. We were both just kinda doing our own thing. Most of my friends never knew he existed, and any who did only knew him by a nickname, but he was in my life longer than almost anyone else.

I want to note that hooking up with someone for the sake of hooking up contradicts the mindset of exclusivity. In many instances I returned to Lyle before things fully ended with other people I really liked, such as York (you'll be hearing about him a lot), because I thought it was over, but then York would come back and I wouldn't know what to do because I felt guilty hooking up with Lyle if York wanted to be with me. I never wanted to overlap the men I was sleeping with but I often prematurely assumed they moved on when they stopped reaching out. There were numerous periods of time in which Lyle was missing from my life, but he was always there.

We still had that shared craving for sex, after all.

***

Reappearances were abrupt, but I always figured he was busy or found a someone new since it was never an exclusivity thing—he was never *obligated* to have sex with me, he *chose* to. When he was in my neck of the woods (all the time), he would ask what time he could see me and stopped by my place if I was available.

After one hiatus, he reached out. This time was different. This time, *he was single*.

That was the day everything changed. He now had a new void to fill—the *emotional* void, which was not available from me. This thing between us worked as long as he had an anchor, but with the anchor no longer hooked to anything, he was drifting. Lyle and I knew each other for years; but this changed everything. He was one of the few constants in my life since moving to the city and now, the dynamics of our agreement and relationship were shifting. What we always had with each other was someone to share the corrupt sides of ourselves with without judgement—sharing dirty sex and stories of drugs, drunk nights, and breaking laws. I could share the devil sitting on my shoulder with him and he was able to share his with me.

Moments with Lyle were just us; naked, sweaty and stoned in a hazy room. The cards were face-up on the table. There was no need to lead anyone on or manipulate each other, we both just wanted to bang, no strings attached. Because his emotional needs were being met elsewhere in the beginning—we never even talked about a relationship as a possibility. Over the years, some red flags disappeared but new ones always presented themselves. It was strictly physical and that was exactly what we both wanted, but over time, it grew to be something else for him.

Avoiding emotions is something that men appear to so effortlessly do, yet every time I tried, I ended up tangled in a web that prevented me from thinking rationally. With Lyle I successfully managed to avoid it. Occasionally, the thought would pop into my head, pondering what our lives would look like if we were to accidentally get pregnant, but I was highly experienced in fighting those thoughts about him by that point since I'd already been doing so for several years. Instead I chose to intensely focus on the reasons why we didn't want to embark in that direction as I continued to search for Mr. Right.

Acknowledging intentions from the start was ultimately the key to how we got where we were; but as we all know, change is the only constant. To be honest, I have no idea when the switch got flipped, but after *years* of going nowhere with each other except for in and out or back and forth, we found ourselves sitting across from each other at a table with a mouthwatering plate of garlicky goodness steaming between us.

It was so… *foreign*. Well, for us anyway.

I felt awkward for the duration of the meal because it felt like sitting there meant something more to him than it did to me. Date-vibes were strong and he was acting just as weird as I was. Neither one of us knew what to do or say; all of the sudden I felt like we were strangers. How did we end up here? Why were we *both* acting this way? Why was I being so quiet? Were we developing feelings for each other after all? Perhaps this whole thing was not our most brilliant idea.

Or maybe, it was.

This is the limbo of the relationship world.

I had no idea what we were doing and neither of us were willing to bring it up. I had no idea how to begin a conversation about emotions or feelings at the time. We saw each other a few times after that, then I stopped agreeing to see him because I had no idea how to tell him how I felt about him. I felt guilty because I could feel that his intentions were different now than they were at first. It was like I couldn't justify having sex anymore with my old mindset and his new intention. After years of hooking up, I was abruptly uninterested.

He became more than just a sex-friend throughout the duration of our relationship. Many women have told me they would never be able to sleep around the way I did, and it turns out neither could I—I was just really good at convincing myself and everyone else that I was. I never had an anchor during those early dating years, so Lyle was the first constant in my life. The consequences of my decision to have sex with Lyle for the wrong reasons wouldn't bring themselves to my attention until I pursued this outlet of therapeutic writing several years later.

LESSON #12
There are always strings attached.

And that's okay; in fact, we should celebrate it.

It is possible to delay the strengthening and tying of said strings before we have to cut them, and THAT'S the journey you're signing up for when you sleep with someone you like right off the bat. There are three simple conditions that must be present at the start for a sex-cessful casual hook-up/friends-with-benefits scenario—

1. Mutual physical attraction/sexual desire/chemistry/magic.
2. Intentions are established <u>BEFORE</u> the first hook up.
3. Both people are disconnected from their emotions.

If any pillar is missing, the entire thing is impossible to construct. If one pillar weakens, stress is placed on the other pillars and the entire thing crumbles to the ground. In an engineering course in college, I learned triangles are the strongest shape. However, no tower can stand forever because nothing in time ever does. Things only remain the same until they are influenced by an outside force. The only thing that lasts forever is the concept of time itself.

Pillars #1 and #2 are simple—it's either there or it isn't. It's purely instinctual and organic. Pillar #3 is weathered and subject to various cracks over time. When even the slightest bit of emotional connection presents itself, the trifecta is impossible to sustain in its original state. We both failed to discuss emotions, so our pillar stayed intact for a long time. I never learned how to; I spent the majority of my time numbing mine. How would it be possible to open up about my feelings to other people when I didn't even acknowledge them to myself?

Many of us are quite good at hiding our feelings and emotions when we want to, and with sex, there are generally feelings by at least one of the two people at any given point, it's normal. It's inevitable. It's supposed to be that way.

We chose the devil *instead* of the angel in the first place. Fire always burns; that's literally it's primary function. Only the "angels" flying above avoid the flames entirely. Can a devil learn to fly? How do we gain clarity amidst emotional haze and achieve divine connection with not only others, but with ourselves?

***

Lyle marked a turning point where I changed my dating mindset and if I waited until later to share it, this book wouldn't make sense. He would be in Part III of this book but he's not because I never wanted to marry him. It's important to understand how much influence he had in my life because this won't be the last time you hear his name. Lyle asked me about an open relationship and I would not agree to that. Ironically, an open relationship would be exactly what I "needed" had I understood my addictions better at the time, but instead I allowed my experience with Edward to hold too much weight on the entire "open" concept.

How on Earth did I expect to find a healthy, *monogamous* relationship while sleeping with or maintaining a relationship with Lyle? It really does sound absurd, but back then, my inexperienced mind justified this to be logical. We were perfectly bad for each other until we weren't, but that's where I was wrong—we were always bad for each other.

Let's return to about a month or so after that Halloween.

*

THIRTEEN

MARTIN

"A man can sleep around, no questions asked,
but if a woman makes nineteen or twenty mistakes she's a tramp."
Joan Rivers

My life was unlike anything I ever imagined.

Every night I was smoking with my friends on my balcony, out drinking at bars with random dudes from the Internet, or doing the bare minimum amount of homework so I could go get drunk with someone else who was just as miserable as I was. I was still looking for "The One;" as many twenty-somethings are, though it had kinda taken a backseat to all the fun I was having.

"Soulmates" are everywhere, it is timing that determines the experiences we have with each other.

All of my friends were getting in new relationships, and it seems like one of every couple's favorite pastimes is meddling in their single friends' love lives. There is usually a reason people are single, and forcefully connecting them with other single people doesn't necessarily change that. It often creates more problems. Have you ever tried setting one of your friends up? Chances are, the sparks you thought would fly never flew.

SINGLE-ITIS—
A mindset explained by the inability to be content alone.

- *Causes include (but are not limited to) not knowing what one wants, feeling unworthy, unaddressed trauma, and lack of self-love*
- *Common symptoms are desperation, neediness, loneliness, substance abuse, and an unhealthy desire to please others*
- *If not diagnosed and treated early, Single-itis can bring forth the complete deterioration of friendships and exclusion from social gatherings, as well as failed relationships and further trauma*
- *In the event of the complete failure of diagnosis, single-itis may result in extremely self-destructive behavior*

I was infected with an extreme case.

Almost all my friends have tried setting me up at some point in time. It never worked for the same reason none of my other relationships worked; <u>I did not understand love nor what I wanted</u>, and these two crucial things would need to be addressed before I would ever truly be capable of loving someone else. While I do sincerely appreciate my friends care about me, I was simply not capable of a meaningful relationship… which means my friends were constantly setting people up with me who would be turned away before they even got their foot in the door.

With that said, Martin was never someone I was interested in. He is part of this story because he was friends with Noah.

***

One of my friends asked me to join her to meet her new man (we'll call those two Minnie and Mick) and a few of his buddies. Mick seemed like a cool dude so I anticipated his friends would be equally as dope. They were.

The live band was playing some folk music and we could hear it from the street before we even made it inside the pub. Minnie and I walked in and wandered around in search of five men I didn't know in a room of almost 100% men. After a couple laps around the place, they spotted us. Mick was holding a set of freshly poured beers and handed one to each of us. The mingling commenced and I was immediately drawn to Noah from the first moment we made eye contact. He was more than just my type. The entire night I noticed that I was inching progressively closer to him... or was he moving progressively closer to me?

We were magnetic.

Each time I found myself standing close enough to Noah to see the sparkle in his eyes, this other guy in the group, Martin, swooped in with another drink and interrupted our conversation, shutting Noah out. By the time the night ended, I was unquestionably drunk; as was my friend. Minnie and I made a stop in the restroom where she handed me the key to her apartment so I could return to grab my things, then drive home from there. She told me she was going to stay with Mick that night and if I wasn't capable of driving, I was welcome to just crash at her place.

"Soooo, what do you think of Martin?" She asked me.

"Eh, he's not my type. But I do really like Noah..."

She warned me about Noah; insisting that Martin was a better match for me. She told me Noah was a huge player. He was definitely attractive enough to claim that title, but it didn't mean anything to me because I didn't know him, and he didn't know me. What if I was a player, too?

Everything about this night felt out of my control. I was not interested in Martin, but Minnie continued to push us together. We made our way outside to the street and I was prepared to call myself an Uber, but Mick was quick to offer Martin's services to drive me back. I was told it was "on the way home for him." [Fun fact: it was in the opposite direction.]

"He's a good guy, I trust him." Mick assured me. I bid farewell to Minnie and the rest of the guys, including Noah, and reluctantly stepped into Martin's car.

"Are you hungry? I'm craving tacos." He asked as he put his hand on my leg and we pulled away from the curb. I was getting a particularly aggressive vibe from him. I was assured I could trust him, but my intuition was telling me something was off. Now I was buckled in to the passenger's seat of his car and I had to ride out my decision.

"No thanks. I'm just ready to go home." I was irritated for two reasons, both *within* my control—First, because he stood in between me and Noah, and second, he was now adding stops between me and my home, the two things I wanted that night. Additionally, the fast food joint he selected gives everyone mad diarrhea, something I also had no desire to deal with.

He ordered himself a few things and continued on to drop me off. He convinced me to get one taco which served as a reminder of just how simultaneously awful and delightful the damn things are. One was all I needed for my butthole to regret it.

I'll pick back up with my friend's keys, which I had just dropped onto the doormat after rummaging around in my purse to locate them. I injected them into the keyhole guided by the light at the end of the hallway. Martin wanted to sit down and eat our food before we parted ways because I was "too drunk to drive." I agreed to disagree; but ultimately he was right.

Immediately upon entering, I compiled my things and set them by the door so if things got weird, I would be ready to bounce. I had a few drinks that night so I was already in a perfect state to make a bad decision, which I did, but thankfully I didn't make the *worst* decision, to have sex with Martin, which I believed would completely decimate any possibility of being with Noah. Martin stuck his tongue as far as he could down my throat that night but I didn't feel a thing because all I could think about was Noah; why was I authorizing Martin to assault my face like this?

You can't force chemistry; just because you feel it doesn't mean someone else does, and vice versa. If two chemicals aren't going to react, they're not going to react. Not everything is going to be baking soda and vinegar or bleach and ammonia. Martin and I were like water and oil. These two things are a disaster when heated together. Look it up, it's science.

He was not my type, and for the sake of being physical, isn't the point to be with someone that excites you? Otherwise, you're thinking about someone else you're into more, which is exactly why I had Noah on the brain. As soon as I felt Martin's hands sliding under the seams of my clothes, I jumped off that couch and told him I needed to leave immediately.

"Aw, really? Just when we were about to start having *fun*?"

"Yes, really. Please, I need you to leave so I can go home."

I knew what he was trying to do, but I was not that girl, not for him. He was not the guy for me because I thought Noah was. All I wanted was Noah. I was so fixated on the idea of being with him after only spending an hour having a conversation over the blaring music of a live band in a tiny pub. I literally experienced a physical feeling in his presence; the same kind of feeling I'd felt with Caleb.

With that said, it was not the feeling I had with Martin.

All Martin did that night was try to get me drunk and feed me the components of butthole lava. That's not the way into my heart and even more so, the *most* obvious way to remain outside of my pants. I'm not completely sure anyone would want to be in there after that.

LESSON #13
Bad decisions are like dominos.

Just one and a whole sequence is going down. Alcohol literally renders us incapable of rational decision making. Being prepared is the best way to help yourself from making further bad decisions when impaired. Always have a backup plan as to how you're going to get home safe if you drink, and develop the plan before you're under the influence.

Despite not being interested in Martin, I still made out with him. I was just making out with guys because it was fun. This perfectly sums up hook-up culture. Addicts only feel normal when they are engaging in their addicted behavior, and in any other moment, they are wishing they were doing it. I was addicted to physical interaction with men—it was more than just sex. I was addicted to the feeling of being desired; desperate for attention.

It would be more in line with what I wanted had I declined the numerous alcoholic beverages Martin kept handing to me but I had yet to actually learn anything about my limits at that point and was just using alcohol to forget. It was my original plan to order an Uber to get home but I gave in to the temptation of a free ride. Allowing Martin to join me inside my friend's apartment provided him an opportunity to make a move on me. It didn't make any sense for me to kiss him back, but I made out with him because for a moment, I just wanted to feel normal, *to feel loved,* albeit anything but. Making out with him conflicted with what I wanted. I wish I handled the night differently. Could have, should have, would have—*had I been sober* and more capable of making *good* decisions, but I wasn't.

As I learned with Dawson, <u>you</u> are the only person who is always going to have your back and your best interests in mind. You know yourself better than anyone else in this world, so take care of YOU first. It's okay to be selfish. *It's okay to say NO!*

Martin was a brief crossing point on the timeline of my life. This night was crucial in learning something much bigger; a lesson for me that was a long time coming.

*

FOURTEEN

NOAH

*"Never allow someone to be your priority while
allowing yourself to be their option."*
Mark Twain

I didn't run into Martin or Noah for months.

The next time we crossed paths, it was New Year's Eve.

My friends and I were dressed to the nines in our flashy
sequence and fancy shoes. We were ready to bring the new year in
with a bang, lots of alcohol, and good people. We strolled into the
venue a couple hours before midnight, alcohol already flowing
through our veins. We paid the entrance fee and were given
wristbands for unlimited beer, wine and champagne. We made our
way over to the bar to get our party started.

Minutes after our arrival, I felt a tap on my shoulder.

I spun around only to be dizzied by Noah himself.

"I didn't know you were going to be here," he murmured in
my ear. Shivers surged down my spine and for a second I forgot
where I was, what I was doing or who he was. Who was I? I was
merely putty in the palm of his hands.

His smile lit up the dimly lit room so fast I was immediately
transported into next year, and all I saw was him. My friends tried

to collect me for bathroom breaks on numerous occasions and I couldn't be bothered; I didn't feel my bladder anyways. I was high in my heels and hallucinating in his presence. Talking to Noah and staring into his eyes made the rest of the world irrelevant. Midnight was about to strike and for the first time in my life on NYE, it felt like everything was falling into place.

Five!

Four!

THREE!

TWOOO!!

OONNEEEEE!

HAAPPYY NEEWW YEAARRRR!

Not a single beat was missed before I felt his lips pressed against mine as the room around us erupted in cheers and screams and excitement and kisses of all kinds. Suddenly, the past was the past. *This* was a fresh beginning. My body was soaring higher than it had ever soared before. Noah and I had the kind of chemistry people dream about, it felt like magic. One kiss was all it took—Dua Lipa was right.

When the bar started shutting down, all the guests were ushered outside to the sidewalk where drunk people were wandering around in the street like zombies, tripping over their own feet and moaning through the onset of their premature hangovers. Out of nowhere a punch was thrown near where I was standing. Noah picked me up and set me down away from the developing street fight, and before I could see where he went, my friend grabbed my arm and pulled me inside a car. I didn't get to say goodbye; Noah never even got my number. My friends were looking out for me, but I was pissed they were getting in my way and I wanted Noah. I was super irritated.

Noah ended up asking Mick for my digits, so it wasn't the last time we saw each other. Our first conversation evolved into a dinner date, then a movie date, and then, we had sex. I spent the night at his place on a handful of occasions, then we'd return back to our everyday lives.

One morning I woke up in his bed and opened my eyes to see Noah looking at dating profiles online and messaging women. I was traumatized. I pretended like I never saw, but it hurt. I felt like I wasn't good enough; he was already looking for the next person to wake up to and I was still there! Did he think I was *ugly*? Was I that unlovable? Or bad at sex? I thought I messed everything up, but we simply lacked an emotional connection and neither one of us were ready for anything serious with each other. One of the primary reasons infant relationships die is if there is no sharing of emotions. He was only interested in opening my legs, and since I wanted him in any way he was willing to give himself to me, I did what I needed to do to please him.

I felt different around Noah; a feeling I mistook for love when in actuality it was a simple physical response my body was having to his—his body was a stimuli, and mine was the same for him.

Question marks swirled around my mind; I could not for the life of me figure out why I wasn't good enough to make him get off dating apps. I went on a few dates before I had sex with him, which was what I thought I needed to do for things to progress (according to the mainstream dating advice I was consuming). My insecurities destroyed all possibility of anything meaningful growing between us. This certainly wasn't the first or last time I let that happen. He soon stopped reaching out to me altogether, meaning I was officially replaced.

For a couple weeks I thought I messed everything up. I wept to my friends on repeat, beating myself up trying to figure out where I went wrong but failed to listen to the actual words they were responding with. This is selective hearing. Soon it wasn't just Noah that was ghosting me, *so were Minnie and several of my other friends*. What was going on?

Gossip of my promiscuous behavior spread like wildfire among the group. Gossiping provides a high for which drama is the hangover. Gossiping is in the same family as smoking or swearing or having sex or gambling, only instead of destroying your lungs or your bank account, the damages are emotional. They are things we say to make us feel better about ourselves temporarily by judging the actions of others. Gossip is a coping mechanism for making the darker sides of ourselves feel less dark.

People talk, they always have and always will.

When I was finally able to get a helpful response from one of the girls, I learned everyone knew I hooked up with both Martin and Noah, then the rest of the guys in that group started throwing themselves at me, too, since there was concrete evidence I was easy. None of the girls in the group wanted to associate themselves with me anymore. I was not mature enough to understand how my behavior looked from their perspective and the influence it had within a group dynamic, nor was I capable of engaging in serious conversations without taking personal offense. My only option at this point was to leave everyone alone since no one wanted to talk to me anyways.

Why did guys I wanted to be with not want to be with me? Why did guys I didn't want to be with want to be with me? Nothing made sense. How and when did I become so big of a problem that even my friends couldn't tolerate me anymore?

It is perhaps one of the most important lessons of all; one that applies to all of us in a world where men and women exist in almost every environment together for the first time in history; we are closer to equality now more than ever before. Noah brought me to a realization that dramatically improved the quality of my life:

<u>LESSON #14</u>
Don't poop where you eat.

There are so many fish in the sea; seriously, just make an online dating account or sit alone in a bar and you'll see what I mean. Do not "hook up" with people from places you regularly spend your time or with those having mutual friends unless you're ready to have a conversation with that person before doing so. I damaged a number of friendships due to my reckless behavior; though there was of course always a partner in the crime.

Not pooping where you eat applies to the following:

- Friend groups
- Work places
- Classroom
- Spiritual places
- Any other place you frequent

These are your "eating places."

But where does one meet their "soulmate?" You may ask? It is totally possible to bump into them in one of these places or on the internet, or literally anywhere. All I am suggesting is that you don't engage in any sort of *sexual* activity with people from any of those main areas of your life <u>unless</u> it first satisfies the following condition:

INTENTIONS ARE DISCUSSED FIRST.

When is it time to have this conversation?

<u>Before anything happens</u>.

Two people must be on the same page about what they want, otherwise the corrupt decision will have a ripple effect of stress in the various mutual aspects of their lives. I wanted a relationship with Noah but led him to believe I just wanted to have sex because that was the behavior I exhibited from the get go. This is what I taught him was an acceptable way to treat me.

We must have conversations with people about our intentions BEFORE becoming physically involved. Communicating our boundaries is essential to any healthy relationship. Noah and I never even had one conversation about a future. We just started having sex one day after a couple dates.

Friends are the family you choose and becoming sexually involved with someone changes a dynamic in a group setting. Friends of friends are still friends. Sex has the power to change everything because *we choose to allow it to.* Hooking up influences dating culture because *we choose to allow it to*. So many times I allowed my sexual relationships to cause problems in all my friend groups over the years; but this had to be the last time.

After I accepted that Noah was never going to see me in a more serious way, I promised myself I would never again become sexually involved with the friends of my friends, and only since that day have I finally been able to nurture and sustain healthy friendships. Crazy how much power sex has, eh?

Let's journey away from the strong O in NOah and onward to the land of Oz... which I will tell you right now is not what it sounds like. I kissed a few others along the way, including Vance and York, who you'll meet much later. The details of their stories are not important at this time, but I actually grew so emotionally invested in York, I even told Lyle I couldn't see him anymore because I thought it would work out. *Spoiler alert* It didn't.

I felt heartbroken. I'll drop you off somewhere near the ending point of that initial fling with York.

By the time I got to Oz, I was a total wreck.

*

FIFTEEN

OZ

"Success is how high you bounce when you hit rock bottom."
George S. Patton

Want to come with me to this food festival?

Damn, he knew exactly how to fast-track his way into my heart. I was looking for a clean place to eat after pooping on the last plate. Food? Um, *yes*. Food FESTIVAL?! *Okay, just marry me already.*

We met at a bar after work for a quick drink to get to know each other a few days before the festival. We were in agreement that we would have a better idea of our compatibility if we met in person to make sure we liked each other as much as we thought we did—it's like a chemistry check. Our brief conversation and introduction went well, but we were there for less than an hour—I spent more time sitting in traffic to get there.

Oz was smart, charming, and had loads of curious things to say. He volunteered to pick me up from my apartment before the event and we would depart from there. He was hardly any more or less of a stranger than he was before we had that drink, but he gave me no reason not to trust him, so I did. It was based simply on the fact that nothing bad happened to me with a stranger from the internet...

Not yet, at least.

We wore our baggiest clothes and stuffed our faces full of literally anything we could get our mouths on. There was ceviche, wings, craft beer, ice cream, tostadas, margaritas, and so much more. Oz held my hand all day long and it all felt so innocent. Every person he talked to smiled when he interacted with them. Every move he made was graceful, he was almost *too* perfect... except he didn't seem to want to talk to me much.

The sun started to set as the event came to a close and Oz gave me a long kiss before we hopped in the car and voyaged home. We were both deep in food coma and made plans to grab drinks with his friends later that week as he dropped me off at my apartment. Nothing else happened between us the day of the festival.

The following week, I met him at a bar in his neighborhood where he was already drinking with his friends. Meeting a group of drunk strangers can be exhausting so I drank a lot more than I typically would when meeting people; I wanted them to like me. After a few drinks, we walked back to his place, which was where my car was parked.

Everything I was doing literally conflicted with my overall goal to make better bad decisions. I was still trying to get York out of my head and probably should not have been out with this guy. This was Ivan and Dawson De-ja-vu, only this time, less alcohol was involved on my end, but an equal amount of preventative measures I could have taken to avoid the predicament altogether. I was on a rebound loop. I was in withdrawal.

"Want a glass of water before you take off?"

TRIGGER WARNING – STRANGER DANGER

Water was a brilliant idea before driving home, but from the moment I stepped into his apartment I felt like something was off and I completely disregarded my intuition. Instead of a glass of water, I wound up with another alcoholic beverage. He put on a random TV show to watch and sat down on the couch, patting the seat next to him as an invitation for me to join him there. It's remarkable how quickly this happened upon entering his dwelling. This obviously wasn't his first time making that move. And last time, it worked, too.

"Where's your bathroom?" I asked. He pointed down the hall. When I was done, I opened the bathroom door to him standing on the other side, blocking the hall back to the living room we were sitting in moments prior. He grabbed my arm.

"Wait, aren't we going to watch that show...?"

He pulled me into his bedroom. I gripped the bedroom door frame and held on; I knew what this was. I told him "no." I told him to stop. I asked him to let me go. I tried breaking myself free from him but gave up. He removed my clothes and had his way with me. I'll spare you the rest.

It was one of the worst nights of my life, but I will admit it was infinitely less humiliating than the Dawson situation because that time, half a dozen people saw me laying on the hardwood floor completely naked and unconscious. Oz took from me what no one else had before—sex completely lost purpose for me after this. It meant nothing. To make matters worse, that night I slept in York's bed; but he had no idea because he was also hammered when I showed up.

LESSON #15
Don't go inside a stranger's home.

To be honest, I feel ridiculous writing that, but in all honesty, there is simply no good reason to go there unless you want to have sex, it is part of your job or you are in attendance of an event. It is important to define and understand what the word *stranger* really means, and who falls into this category.

The definition provided by the dictionary is as follows:

"a person whom one does not know"

The question then becomes, *At what point do you truly know someone?* I invited Harold and Lyle inside my apartment after meeting them once. Ivan was just as much of a stranger to me but because we grew up in the same town, I didn't *consider* him to be one. I knew nothing about Martin or Noah, they were just as strange as any of the others, but they were both friends of a friend of a friend of mine. How do we become *more* than strangers?

Strangers are just acquaintances we haven't met yet; and acquaintances are merely friends we haven't connected with yet. When you can honestly say you know someone, you are able to predict how they will behave, and until you are able to do that, you know nothing. This typically comes with time and bonding moments.

Why didn't I consider Oz to be a stranger? We had no connection; in fact, I could hardly get him to talk to me at all so I knew nothing about him; I never even knew his last name. He could have killed me and no one would even know what happened to me. It takes more than a few drinks with someone to *know* them, but I was too naïve to understand that. I thought that he would have kidnapped, killed, or had his way with me the day of the festival if that was the type of person he was, but it was only <u>after</u> I let my guard down that it happened.

I longed for a friend to open up to about the experience, but friends were something I no longer felt I had. All my friendships were in shambles because I pushed everyone away and gave my addictions complete control over my life. There was no one for me to turn to except for myself. I was getting raped, emotionally abused, ghosted, ignored, and used because I never once took a moment to sit down and address my past trauma. *I had to start there.*

I was lost, alone, intoxicated and drowning in a pool of my own tears; I lacked the courage required to acknowledge and reflect upon my own decisions so that I would be able to go through metamorphosis; and only then would I be able to break free of the cocoon I imprisoned myself in. The only thing I could think to do at the time was to continue swiping; hoping my Prince Charming would reveal himself to me. My dreadful habits were showing their true colors and they weren't pretty.

There was no love left in my heart for myself, let alone anyone else. My self-worth was so low and I was so lonely I even stayed in contact with Oz, begging for his attention. I had no self-respect, no self-love, and no one to trust, not even myself. Shortly after this, I even ended up kissing Martin again. How do you pick yourself back up after hitting rock bottom?

You just do. It's actually the sturdiest place to build from.

*

SIXTEEN

PRESTON

*"Insanity is doing the same thing over and over again
and expecting different results."*
Unknown

My last few attempts to find love proved to be far more painful than I thought as I was out of the game for a couple months, but I returned to home plate ready to start swinging at anything that was thrown at me. I went through hell and now I was back. "Take things slow," was the advice people kept giving me, and maybe they were right. Was I moving too fast with *everyone* I wanted to be with? My friends convinced me that unless there was a commitment or label, I should continue to date other people. One even compared it to farming—

"Just date around and plant a bunch of seeds! Then in a couple years you'll reap the benefits of the harvest."

Is that actually good advice? (You'll find out in Part III.)

Perhaps sex was the devil after all, and if I refrained from having it, *then* I would then find love? It was time to try something new—a method of abstinence. I told myself I would refrain from sleeping with the people I dated at least until they asked me to be their girlfriend, which, *spoiler alert,* never happened. It was back to the apps for me.

I'm pretty good at running in heels too.

My profile mentioned that I could run in high heels and Preston's first message confirmed he read it. I contemplated how to respond while I tossed my clothes into the machine at the laundromat.

"Let's race." I responded.

> *I won't let you win. I respect you too much for that.*
> *What are you running away from?*

It's like he already knew me.

Preston was dashingly handsome and exceptionally witty. His entire profile was littered with personality from his punny tagline to his goofy faces and thrilling travels. He had a sense of humor and was just an all-around, positive person. Our initial conversation was playful and we set up a time and place to meet before I even finished drying my clothes. Let's fast forward to that date—

***

"Wow, you look gorgeous." He was sitting at a high top table in the back of the bar drinking some sort of dark liquor.

"Thanks." I blushed and took a seat across from him on the bench against the wall. His perfect smile sent waves of electricity down my spine and my heart racing into overdrive. The conversation flowed like a river. It was the first time I felt like I was connecting with someone since I met York.

We looked at the clock and realized that our minutes together flew by a million times faster than we anticipated; we both had other places to be. Plans were made before I walked out the door to go bowling the following week, *but* we enjoyed each other's company so much we grabbed dinner one day before then as well.

***

"I got a strike!" He picked me up and kissed me in the middle of the bowling alley. All the trauma I endured up to this point was for something better; it was so that I could do things right with Preston. I was smitten. So smitten, in fact, that I again told Lyle that I couldn't see him anymore for the first time since York.

Preston introduced me to his brother, his roommates, and all his friends. I was surprised this guy was already familiarizing me with some of the most important people in his life, but I was delighted. He was taking a chance on me. Something was different.

For about a month, we were hanging out all the time. Comedy shows. Bars. Bowling. Video games. He texted me first thing in the morning, he texted me right before he went to bed at night. The only two things we didn't have yet were sex and a label; which were two things I considered to determine a relationship. This disregards the MOST important thing, which is understanding each other's intentions. Those two other things can be the most harmful things to the success of a relationship because we are valuing *things* above the *person* we are sharing them with. Why was I so fixated on those words?

After a month, he wanted to take things to the next level physically but I had yet to receive the type of commitment I required from him before we took that step. We were friends but still didn't know that much about each other. I was not in the right headspace for dating. I didn't know what to tell him, I couldn't even open up about my past because I wasn't ready to accept it and I feared if I opened my mouth enough to tell him why I didn't want to have sex yet, he would walk away. Turns out that's exactly what happened anyway.

One evening, he made a move, something that would normally excite me, but instead of opening my legs, I sealed them shut and to make matters worse, I emotionally shut down, too. He tried to figure out what was going on but I was a lost cause because I wouldn't let anyone in. I was triggered by everything because of my unaddressed trauma. He even asked if I was a virgin. (Lol.)

He offered to help pull me out of the emotional hole I dug myself and I slapped his metaphorical hand away. I thought if he found out that I was carrying all this baggage, he'd abandon me like everyone else, I was sure of it. Eventually he stopped trying to help me feel comfortable opening up about the subject. *Then*, he left. I gave him no choice other than to give up—my walls were simply too high.

I wanted to try to make it work but I was holding back by following the advice of my friends and dating coaches from the internet; I wanted to find love but my walls were so high no one could even figure out what was on the other side. Preston was kind, patient, and respectful. He spent time getting to know me *without* sex as he had been doing so for weeks. I sabotaged it because I didn't think I deserved him.

LESSON #16
Abstinence reveals intentions.

Exercising abstinence isn't a religious thing, it's something we do to respect ourselves and differentiate between someone who cares about us from those who objectify us. It acts like a filter. With that said, abstaining usually also means you are holding yourself back from doing something you still want (and intend) to do, making it incredibly difficult unless you are able to shift your mindset and control your physical being. Abstinence is a matter of self-discipline.

Preston and I were a month deep in memories and had yet to do anything other than kiss each other. I was so busy overthinking the entire thing and trying to calculate the right series of actions and things to say to keep him in my life instead of just putting my intentions out into the universe and trusting it. I was incapable of communicating what I wanted to him—which I now realize is because I had no idea what that was.

Our connection dissipated because I failed to open myself up to him. I had major trust issues. I wanted to avoid feeling pain and weakness; and I knew talking about my emotions would amplify them and result in reliving the same events I wanted to forget. I assumed Preston was just trying to get in my pants and that he would discard me as soon as he did.

In most cases, a person who introduces you to their friends, spends time getting to know you, and makes plans to spend real time with you wants more than just sex. I wanted him to ask me to be his girlfriend first because I needed to feel secure, but I never expressed that to him. I just expected him to read my mind. Why did I *need* that commitment from him before having sex? He would never be able to fix the real issue, my void for love, anyway.

Voids are the reason anyone believes they "need" anything. By definition, a void is "an empty space." *Need* is one of the most overused words in the English language. We say we *need* coffee, we say we *need* chocolate, we say we *need* to cuddle with our dog. We *need* cigarettes, we *need* God, we *need* to post on social media, we *need* new clothes. We *need* to be there 5 minutes early. We *need* to wait til tomorrow. And so on. ALL of these things are merely desires, not needs. Replace the word *need* with <u>*want*</u> and your entire life will change. The only things we all truly need as humans are food, water, shelter, and love. These are the <u>only</u> things required to maintain life at its most basic level.

With that said, do we *need* sex?

YES!

...But only for the purpose of continuing the human race. For all other reasons, no. We don't *need* sex. We *want* sex because there are rewards (climax and connection). I'm not saying there's a problem with wanting sex, but there are so many issues that arise from doing it for the wrong reasons and failing to discuss intentions ahead of time.

Preston watched me break down, much like I watched Kurt a year prior. I was emotionally bleeding and he offered to help, but I pushed him away. I knew I wasn't his problem to fix, I was mine; I got myself into this hole and had to figure out how to climb out of it. He then "ghosted" me, which I attributed to not having sex with him. It was back to crying and entertaining my various addictions to cope with the loss. *Why was having sex such a major turning point?*

I still couldn't figure it out, but I was on to something.

*

SEVENTEEN

QUENTIN

"If you think you're too small to make a difference,
try sleeping with a mosquito in the room."
Dalai Lama

After the loss of York, my unfortunate visit to Oz, and now the sudden disappearance of Preston, I fell into the deep end. I felt alone in a world of people closed off to intimacy but that's a bold statement considering I was perhaps the worst of all. Anytime someone with good intentions walked into my life, I sabotaged it.

For weeks I cried in my bedroom wasting precious daylight staying miserable, I removed myself from apps and focused on my college degree. During this time, many of my friends started to fade out of my life. For years I was ruthlessly dating and devaluing my loved ones by spending my free time meeting more temporary people, so I suddenly had time and attention voids to fill.

Thankfully, it was around this time I reconnected with an old friend of mine who was also going through a break-up and she helped me in ways relating to living a healthier life all-around. She opened my mind to the importance of purging negativity from various areas of my life from the food I consumed, to the people I chose to spend my time with, to regular exercising, to where I directed my attention, to meditating, and so on. Only once I started to adopt these healthier habits would I have room for things that *add* value to my life rather than obliterate it. I was not in a good place, but one of the most beautiful things about the universe is that if you have the courage to put yourself out there, what you need will find its way to you naturally.

I was forced to start looking at things from another perspective. I was determined to pinpoint exactly what was preventing me from finding love. After a month of crying, I wiped the tears off my face and exposed it to the sunshine again. My "soulmate" and I would never find each other if I never left my bedroom.

***

Quentin looked adorable with his arms wrapped around a baby tiger in one of his profile photos. After a lighthearted conversation on the app, we set a date to meet up and despite living a half hour's drive away, he volunteered to make the trek to my hood and even took the initiative to research a bar in my area for us to meet at.

The following weekend, we saw each other again. Then again a few days later. And again. He was a runner like the new me. We were both having such a good time, we weren't even thinking about sex. All signs were pointing in one direction and I couldn't be happier.

About a month passed and I was exercising the same restraint I had with Preston, but after one particularly long night of drinking, he wanted to have sex and I didn't turn him down. The following moments sent me into immediate panic. For the first time in my life, I was faced with one of the most taboo questions of all time—

<u>Does size matter?</u>

Why does it matter if size matters or not? If you believe it does, in fact, matter, does size matter *because* you believe sex matters? Would size matter if the pleasure you got from sex did not exist? Men cannot *choose* the size and shape of their extremities just as women do not select their breast size, though women often do opt to change or mutilate theirs. How ironic is it that we feel a need to change our exterior because we feel inferior on the interior?

If you truly love someone and if someone truly loves you, something so far out of your control won't be a factor in the way they treat you. Would you choose to not love someone because they have an imperfect nose? Or two different sized boobs? Or a giant mole on their face?

"Conditional love" is not love.

On one hand, I was falling for Quentin. He was a great communicator, upbeat, positive, hard-working and ambitious. We shared a lot of the same values and wanted many of the same things out of life. Despite all the things we had going for us, I immediately decided what was happening wasn't going to work out because I was not satisfied with what I discovered in the bedroom. Sex with him changed everything for *me*, not him, and it was in this moment that I realized just how corrupted I was. I felt more shallow than a puddle.

If sex was important enough to be a requirement, why was I wasting time "dating" by getting to know people in the first place? How messed up is it to hold something against someone when it is completely out of their control?

I didn't know what to do; I'd never been in this situation before. I didn't want to tell him the truth but I respected him too much to lie; the ultimate paradox. I felt evil. In an effort to make peace with the idea of breaking it off with him, I slowly pulled away and prayed he would follow suit since most of the other people I dated did that after having sex. This phenomenon is described as "bread-crumbing," or responding with the fewest words possible and never initiating conversation, almost like a drawn out version of ghosting.

He called me out, and to make matters worse, I was so immature I ignored him. I simply couldn't fathom the idea of never sleeping with anyone else ever again, I was in no way ready to give that up. It would never be the same as it was with so many others.

How I treated Quentin I wouldn't wish upon anyone. I am so thankful he called me out as to prevent me from treating anyone else that way ever again. If you love someone, it doesn't matter what the dimensions of their body are. We spent loads of time together and everything fell apart as soon as our clothes fell off. I decided immediately that this abstinence thing was never going to work for me. Objectifying our romantic interests is perhaps the worst way to treat one another. He forced me to reevaluate everything I was doing.

LESSON #17
Size matters if sex matters.

SIZE MATTERS if you believe an orgasm from sex depends on the size and shape of a man's penis. SEX MATTERS if you believe the pleasure someone else can bring you from intercourse is important.

<u>SIZE DOES NOT MATTER</u> if you know how to have an orgasm. <u>SEX DOES NOT MATTER</u> if you unconditionally love someone.

When you love someone, you accept them for how they are. You want them to be a part of your life regardless of the fleshy vessel they were born into. You will only know if you want to spend a lifetime with someone once you get to know their soul; not the extremities of the skin it's in. If this is something you disagree with, you are currently incapable of loving unconditionally. If you are dependent on your partner for pleasure, it will be an unhealthy relationship.

Caring about penis size is a major insecurity for a lot of men, even some of those that I would consider well-endowed. If women *care* about a man's penis size (or any other body part), they do not love them unconditionally. Same goes for us ladies—breast alterations, butt implants, thigh gaps, nose jobs, make-up and so on. Anyone who shares a negative opinion or makes another person feel small because of something they have no control over is probably insecure about the exact thing they are using to hurt you. None of that stuff matters; we must stop feeding ourselves the idea that it does. If anyone outwardly makes a negative comment about another's appearance, it is a direct reflection of their own thoughts and how they feel about themselves. They likely do not love themselves in a healthy way and are projecting their insecurities onto their reality.

No one is perfect; our differences are the exact features that make us all beautiful. The standards we live by today are the collective result of centuries of social conditioning. These ideals are advertised to be important by the same people that are benefitting from them. To be happy in our own skin we must stop comparing ourselves to each other and our ludicrous beauty standards. In today's society, insecure men are led to believe if they aren't getting their lady to climax, it's because they're not suited in that department, but size has nothing to do with it. Female orgasms do not require penetration.

Have you ever watched a documentary about animals mating in the wild? It provides a pretty fascinating perspective into how sex exists in its natural state. The human race exploited the activity for benefits of control, pleasure, and profit.

In my experience, most men only require a few minutes of high intensity, well-lubricated friction to ejaculate, (assuming he is indeed aroused). It is designed to be a fast process because that is all that is necessary for procreation. If the male half of the species had to keep a woman tied down for an hour to get her pregnant, we'd be living in a much kinkier and less-populated world; and honestly, that might be the direction we're headed in. But don't you think it's biologically designed to be a quick process for a reason?

Because I thought sex mattered, that was where I had to start, *but I already tried that!* That was how things started with several others... but nothing ever came from that other than them. I knew I was running away from the truth, but I didn't realize that meant I was also running in circles.

If sex was going to be a determining factor in who I choose to be a lifelong partner, I would have to do it as soon as the guy initiated it. This was a major step in the wrong direction following my abstinence phase. I vowed to myself not to connect with the men I dated emotionally so long as I considered sex to be of importance. How ridiculous is it to abstain from sex until marriage only to have penis size be a make-it or break-it element? Would I get married then divorced after a honeymoon because of a penis?

The downward spiral continued. At this point it became abundantly clear to me that I had an alarming amount of issues, though I had no idea what they all were. The message from the universe kept getting louder and louder. Lovers were actually asking me what was wrong with me and I didn't know how to respond.

For the next six months, I spent the majority of my time working, running, studying and sleeping. I wanted to focus on my school so I would be able to level up in my life.

Around this time, Lyle and I started to hang out *outside* the bedroom. I could feel the circumstances changing, though my feelings did not. Morally, I couldn't justify dating new people the way I had been and I stopped looking for something serious altogether, therefore entering into the incredibly dangerous territory of the one-night stand.

*

EIGHTEEN

RONNIE

"Do not be too timid and squeamish about your actions.
All life is an experiment. The more experiments you make the better"
Ralph Waldo Emerson

My friend Regina invited me to join her at the club to celebrate her coworker's Rhianna's birthday. I rummaged through my closet for something sexy enough to command the attention I craved—an opportunity to fill the sexual void.

The three of us walked straight past the line to the bouncer and into the club like we owned the place. Almost immediately upon entering, a charming, messy-haired boy made eye contact with me and waved to me like he knew me, then made his way in my direction. He invited us to join his table, lit by firepit and fully stocked with more alcohol than any of us would ever be capable of consuming in one night.

After exchanging names and some flirty conversation, we were granted the opportunity to share their private bar with them for the rest of the evening. Regina abruptly split off from the group to be with some guy she was seeing, but Rhianna and I stayed with the boys around the fancy firepit. My gaze was fastened on something other than the drinks and the flames; the eyes of the messy-haired boy who waved to me. Ronnie knew what he wanted and all I knew was that I wanted to know Ronnie.

Not even an hour after arriving, Regina took off with her guy, leaving me and the birthday girl on our own for the night. A couple hours passed and I turned around to see Rhianna lounging on the couch making out with one of Ronnie's friends; a delightful birthday gift to her from the universe. When the lights came on at closing time, Ronnie also lit up with an idea.

"Have you ever been to a strip club?"

"No..."

"Let's go. I'll show you."

Ronnie's idea was so spontaneous that I couldn't refuse; and Rhianna was equally as curious as I was, so we went as a group. Visiting a strip club was on my bucket list, though I always imagined it would be a *male* strip club, not the traditional female kind, but heck, why not? What *does* the inside of a strip club look like? Is it really just women dancing seductively and walking around naked? Are men actually throwing cash money all over the place? I took pole-dancing lessons at one point in my twenties with Regina and even considered becoming a stripper. Could I actually see myself making money doing something like this? I wanted to see for myself.

We piled into the Uber like sardines with a couple of Ronnie's friends. It was a tight fit for four fully grown adults in the back but we were so drunk and giggly no one cared. I was sitting on Ronnie's lap, who by this point already had his hands grasping my lady parts like fresh produce from the farmer's market. To the strip club we went!

***

The bouncers at the club gave the two of us girls a peculiar look as we walked up to the door.

"They're with us." Ronnie said with authority.

Inside we went, wandering through a series of curtains and into an enormous, dimly lit room with a few floor-to-ceiling silver poles on a stage set a few feet above the rest of the floor. The rest of the room was filled with small round tables and loads of chairs. Only about a dozen had people sitting in them.

Half-naked females meandered around the room flirting with the males; some drooled and others looked as though they were uncomfortable being there at all, but everyone was minding their own business. No one was talking. One of the women climbed onto the stage and did a brief, seductive pole dance before collecting a few bills that were tossed on the stage by a man sitting nearest her. This enabled her to determine who was attracted to her so she knew where to direct her efforts.

Ronnie bought his friend a lap dance from one of the women walking about the room, then leaned over and whispered in my ear, "Come with me." Shivers went down my spine.

Although I had no idea where we were going, my curiosity was enough motivation for me to follow. If anything, I could be assured this was a safe place for women, they were comfortable basically walking around naked and that takes guts. I had nothing to worry about. He collected his "favorite stripper" on the way; a brunette. Was he a regular here? I won't go into detail as to what happened in the back room, but he enjoyed every moment of it and while I can't say the strip club is for me, it was worth the experience. Needless to say, I have no intention of returning.

After that enlightening affair we returned to the main room where one of his friends was literally falling asleep in the corner; it was probably three or four in the morning. Ronnie and I were still full of energy like a couple of Energizer Bunnies. After organizing the rest of our friends' routes home, he accompanied me back to my apartment since neither of us were ready to call it quits and it turned out we were neighbors, too.

The following evening we grabbed dinner, and after the weekend concluded, we didn't contact each other again. Technically that means we had a *two*-night stand, which is the same thing, just twice as meaningless. Our connection was short and sweet. What could I possibly learn from Ronnie after knowing him for only 48 hours?

LESSON #18
Nudity is only a big deal if you make it so.

Nakedness and the human body are nothing to be afraid of. He taught me to get out of my comfort zone. It started with his mating call at the bar, the flaunting of cash like a tail of peacock feathers, the locking of eyes and a subtle invitational wave to migrate in his direction. We explored each other's minds and allowed the alcohol to take us into the oblivion. We then strayed to a place where we explored each other's bodies and more, then ended the night together in a bed, naked and unafraid. It unfolded so naturally, we were nothing but animals, and it was incredible.

Humans in today's society have been culturally bred to be either turned on or offended by nudity and by doing so, we've *created* a desire, market and industry for it, *not* the other way around as we are led to believe. Does sheltering the human body actually prevent people from wanting to have sex or does it create more of an appetite for it? If I put a bunch of your favorite cookies in a jar and told you not to touch it, what would you want to do? People will pay money to see an unclothed body or have sex with one (where available). Sex scenes are inserted into movies and people with a lack of imagination pay for pornography to aid in their masturbation. In advertising, everything from food to sports to travel can be sexualized to stimulate a carnal desire within the consumer.

Nature is truly fascinating. There are two different forms of bodies we are born into—male and female—for a reason. Through years of conditioning and sheltering, modern culture either sexualizes or cringes at the very presence of excessive bare skin. Because we've gone through great effort to shield our physical being from the eyes of others, we are more self-conscious about it, and individuals who choose to diverge from this norm immediately become the topic for conversation by all those triggered by it.

There's a lot of money in the sex industry; and people will pay a lot of money for a solution when they believe they have a problem that needs to be solved, regardless of whether that need is real or invented. *Condoms. Birth control. Lube. Toys. Porn. Prostitution. Strip clubs. Dating. Travel. Beauty. Clothing/Fashion. Music. TV. Movies. Books (even this one).* By nature, sex exists to create offspring, but the human species has given sex a second purpose; one of exploitation. We found a way to have more of it without the side effect of creating an embryo.

The simple act of having sex made me feel like I had some control over my dating life and emotions since I never actually had any to begin with. I enjoyed the freedom of the one-time hook-up despite how unsafe it was. To be honest, I think the risk made it that much more appealing to me. Ronnie was not the first nor the last. Feeling wanted and frequently chased by someone new filled the void; it wasn't even about an orgasm anymore.

*

NINETEEN

SIMON

"Better a thousand times careful than once dead."
Proverb

"Want to go to Vegas tomorrow?" My friend Silvia asked one Friday evening after work.

"Heck yes" was my immediate response. Vegas was a great place for me to make better bad decisions and potentially meet a better bad boy. We had the bright idea to drive there and back in 24 hours but we first had to survive the six-hour drive. How much trouble would I manage to get myself into this time?

The following day, we woke up early, packed up the car, and were out the door by mid-morning. We were prepared for just about anything Vegas could throw at us. We pulled up to the hotel with a car full of empty coffee cups, fast food garbage, and bladders at max-capacity. It was time to get this party started.

We changed into our evening attire, touched up our makeup and waltzed downstairs to the casino to get the dice rolling and the drinks pouring. What would the night have in store for us? We had a few ideas.

Silvia's friend got us into one club where a big DJ was performing. We grabbed dinner and some drinks and were on our way. This was surely going to be one of those wicked crazy Vegas nights I would never forget; or as said by many before me, one I would never fully remember. Within seconds of walking into the bar, some guy was already asking one of the other girls for her number. Being a female in Las Vegas is like being a fish in a sea of hungry sharks. We had to swim together or we were going to get bit... I did.

Simon swooped me up from the dance floor and the rest of the girls followed. He had a table on the second level with a view of stage where the DJ stood overlooking the entire dance floor. I was mildly attracted to him but it was too loud to find out much else about the guy. He offered us alcohol and we mingled with his friends, dancing the night away on their personal balcony above the crowds while growing steadily more intoxicated. Before long, Simon and I were lip-locked.

Chemistry was basically inevitable in my drunken state. Sex was predictable. The person I was having sex with didn't even matter to me anymore as long as I was having it. Like drinking—my problem was once I reached the bottom of my glass, I *needed* a new one to fill the void. It was like I was programmed that way.

Silvia tapped me on my shoulder—

"We're leaving, are you ready to go?"

"Stay with me, I'll bring you back to your friends later," Simon shouted in my ear over the music. My phone was looking good on battery life and it wasn't too late, so I nodded.

"Go without me."

The girls left and we continued dancing for a few more songs before wandering out to the casino where we were able to have a conversation. There are no fitting opportunities for talking inside clubs, loud music is one reason why people hook up but never stay hooked; it dissuades visitors from truly connecting with each other so they keep returning to spend money and make more empty connections. After finally getting to know a little about him, losing a few hands of Black Jack and a consuming a few more drinks, we ventured to his room (which was at a completely different hotel).

The suite was on the top floor with a view overlooking the entire Las Vegas strip in all its glowing glory. The bright lights certainly support the idea that no one in Sin City sleeps much, if at all. We certainly didn't get more than a few minutes.

***

BEEP BEEP BEEP BEEP BEEP BEEP

My phone was going off and I rolled over to find myself still naked in Simon's bed. I literally had no recollection of what happened after we got back to the hotel. Silvia was calling me and it wasn't even 7am yet. I jumped up and rummaged through the mountain of clothes and blankets on the floor to silence the demonic screams. I learned to always leave the volume on my phone turned up when staying overnight with random guys.

"Hey, is everything okay?" She asked.

"Yeah. Heading back to the room now. See ya soon." This was the one night stand that influenced not only my dating habits, but my life forever. It would be a while before I understood exactly what the consequence of sleeping with Simon was. They say what happens in Vegas stays in Vegas… except for Herpes; apparently that follows you the rest of your life. I didn't get the Herps from Simon nor did I get preggers, but I did get a different kind of wake-up call.

Simon walked me down to the lobby, gave me a kiss on the forehead and ordered a taxi for me from the front desk. "Let's hang out tonight if you're still around." As soon as the door shut behind me, I was already looking up his name on the internet to find out who he was and where he came from. *And* if there was any chance for us to end up together considering we lived in different states. I was already falling down the rabbit hole and needed to grab a root before I fell too deep. Why did I always do this?

I never saw Simon again. A true one-night stand.

***

A few months later, I went in for STI testing because my menstrual cycles were irregular. For the first time in my life, the test came back positive for something… Chlamydia. I immediately reached out to Lyle and the person I was seeing at the time, William, to inform them so they could get tested as well. Fortunately, Chlamydia is treatable so long as it is caught early, but it has the power to completely destroy a woman's capability to reproduce if left undetected long enough, and since it was almost a year since my last test, I didn't know where it came from or how long I had it. Back then, a lot of guys didn't want to wear a condom since I was on birth control, but I always did on one-night stands.

The damages were amassing and I continued to ignore them. The baggage was a burden beyond what I could ever ask someone to help me carry. Would anyone ever love me given my countless flaws, the colossal magnitude of baggage I was dragging around, and now *this*? My addiction issues and alcohol again were my partners in crime, meaning this entire scenario was preventable.

Whether we used protection or not, I'll never actually know where I caught it from. I'm Patient Zero in my reality so it doesn't really matter. Some STIs are not detectable in men and many don't have symptoms at all, so how can I blame anyone? I may not have gone through the traditional sex-ed course, but I still knew better.

LESSON #19
Always wear a condom. ALWAYS!

It only takes one time to catch a disease, and it only takes one disease to change your life. Birth control is a deceiving solution because we associate it with not getting pregnant. Birth control makes the act of having sex a pleasure-only experience by hormonally preventing the body from accomplishing the biologically intended purpose of organic sexual intercourse—*AN OFFSPRING!*

Upon the realization that condoms were a requirement for my own protection, I went off birth control immediately. If a condom was a necessity to sleep around, taking the pill made no sense. The female body experiences emotional and physical consequences as symptoms of hormonal birth control and there's straight up no way that stuff is good for us. I felt emotionless on birth control—this is going to sound nuts, but I probably only cried a dozen times throughout the five-ish years I was on it. That's not right. Several months after I stopped, I actually had feelings again, I felt like I got my ambition back, and my skin cleared up. Problems I was dealing with disappeared like magic. It was bizarre. When did I decide all those side effects were acceptable? I never noticed how it changed my body until I stopped.

In a dating culture where men believe they are programmed to *need* sex, women pretty much have the opportunity to have sex with whomever they want, whenever they want. However, as Peter Parker's uncle once said, "With great power comes great responsibility," and sex is no exception. Since the beginning of time, it's been *too* easy for women to have sex.

Imagine a world where all the women are infertile due to an STI epidemic or through generations of repeated hormonal birth control. It's farfetched, sure, but after decades of the human race becoming incapable of or choosing not to have children, we may face major population issues. What if our species becomes dependent on the meeting of frozen eggs and sperm of past generations in a Petri dish? That's a bit extreme, I know, but *what if?* Should we be thinking about this as a species? We're all human, after all, and our one common goal is to continue the existence of our species and create a better world for the generations that follow us. Birth control pills, patches and implants cannot seriously be good for our bodies—we are kidding ourselves if we believe otherwise. Humans are the most intelligent species on this planet and we are fully capable of destroying ourselves.

How and why did people become so promiscuous in the first place? We (the human species) never *needed* condoms or birth control before, so why do we *need* condoms and birth control now?

The truth is, we don't *need* any of those things because we don't *need* sex. We choose to have sex because by nature it is designed to feel good so we'll want to do it, and reproduce in the process. When we feel we *need* a temporary moment of pleasure, we don't *need* another body, we only *need* a hand or a toy. Getting sexually involved is an emotional roller coaster, and not wearing a condom is like neglecting to buckle the seatbelt. Even if you think you're being safe by wearing a condom, unexpected things can still happen. Remember Adrian?

One night stands are great fun but are ultimately a terrible idea. I had enough of them to know they're not worth the risk or reward. It leaves you with nothing but emptiness and a temporary high. You have no idea who the other person is or where they've been. There's a reason they emphasize the importance of condoms in sexual education, but since I never took the course, Simon was mine.

I'm the one who made my bed and now I had to lie in it.

**

For the following year and a half I focused on school, so there's a gap of time here. Here's a quick summary...

I met William immediately after Simon and Xerxes about a year later right before Teodoro. I also maintained contact with Lyle and Vance throughout. York reconnected with me right after my graduation.

*

TWENTY

TEODORO

"Honesty prospers in every condition of life."
Friedrich Schiller

This is the kind of story people *think* you experience when you are a single female. And I'll tell you, these epic, spontaneous, beautifully romantic nights do exist outside of fairytales—only, not without all the other stuff you've been reading up to this point. Memorable experiences like the ones you are about to read are few and far between. If you want the good, you have to accept the bad—it's a package deal.

***

Having recently graduated, I was heading to Europe to celebrate like the Germans do. I was taking full advantage of my newfound free time and the money I was making at my new job. Neglecting my social life for a couple years was about to radically pay off.

The night before my flight, York visited me from out of town and I also briefly reconnected with William; *and* I was lusting over Xerxes, a new face that found me when I wasn't looking. I then hooked up with someone from Germany before meeting Teodoro on the same trip. And somehow with all that going on, I was hoping I would finally meet the one guy that could solve all my problems and be my husband one day. Looking back I would consider myself to be pretty delusional.

Strangers provide us with a unique opportunity to start over. When you understand the world is a mirror, you can choose to only see the best in people, and in return they will only see the best in you—though we must also keep in mind that words have different meanings to different people. We see what we choose to focus on. Have you ever considered what impact you make on people you meet? Or what impact you *want* to have? Sometimes, strangers become more than strangers, but before I introduce you to those guys here's a couple more that didn't.

***

Every seat on the train was occupied and when I finally found mine, it was the last one open at a table with a group of French girls who were gossiping about something in their native tongue, I'm not sure because *je ne sais pas parler français* (I don't speak it). French was my least favorite subject in high school because I was horrible at it, I even had a tutor. Thankfully I was heading towards the perfect city to generate a new memory to correspond with the language.

For the majority of the train ride, I was doing that bobbing thing where my head was falling, falling, falling; then suddenly, I'd snap back into consciousness; head flying upwards like a rocket ship blasting off into space; and after adjusting the way I was sitting to one with better posture, my eyelids once again would struggle to remain open, then fall, fall, fall and the process repeated itself.

At one point I woke up with drool running down my arm to the sounds of giggling French teenagers. Falling in love *on the train to* Paris was never in my forecast and that was one of the few things on my trip that went according to plan. I moved seats after the first stop and woke up next to a large man drooling even more than me. It was nice to drool in good company.

When the train finally stopped at the station, it was hours after dark. My sole goal was to find my hostel and pass out. I was formerly at Oktoberfest, then in Amsterdam, so I was drained from all the partying. I gathered my bags and stumbled outside to wait for a taxi.

***

"Merci!" I bid farewell to my non-English speaking driver, proud that I had vocalized one of my first French words on its home soil. I wandered down the dark alley and felt an immediate burst of energy surge through my veins. This wasn't the end of my night, this was only the beginning, and just like that, my adrenaline kicked in and I was ready for just about anything.

After checking in to my room at my hostel and getting some suggestions from the front desk, I sat down and began researching how I was going to utilize my single full day in the magnificent city. Only about ten minutes passed before one of my dorm-mates entered.

"Hey roomie! How's the bar downstairs? Have you spent any time there?" It wasn't long before I discovered she, too, was at Oktoberfest just days before with the same tour company. Our instant connection led to us putting on our shoes and heading out the door to find out what was going on at the hostel bar. Solo travelers all tend to have one major thing in common—we're usually up for anything.

With a pint of beer fresh from the tap in my hand, the night began. My roomie and I were talking to an older European gentleman, a guy from Morocco and a group of dudes from Greece. Everyone spoke English (as most Europeans do). And then, Teodoro joined us. My eyes instantly turned googly.

Teodoro was not French, but he was foreign nonetheless. He was traveling around the world, documenting what he could, and still had a long list of things to accomplish before returning to his native country. He was working small, local jobs for income, so it wasn't a total vacation. He was hard-working and highly curious.

Midnight was inching closer and everyone knew the hostel bar would be closing, but Teodoro knew the area well as he'd been in Paris for a few months already. My hostel roommate and our new group of friends embarked towards a club down the road and had a few more drinks while we danced the night away and bonded over our free-spirits. After a couple hours, Teodoro and I wandered back to the hostel courtyard and sat down on a bench in the dark. We whispered out there about things we've seen, felt, and experienced throughout our journeys until the sky began to reflect the glow of the sun's anticipated arrival in the distance.

"I have to leave so I can get some sleep before work." He gave me a few recommendations for the day and his contact information, not knowing whether or not we would have an opportunity to see each other, and he was gone with the night. I had a lot to accomplish in Paris during my brief stay, so I definitely needed to get some rest, too. Almost ten hours passed since I was bobbing in and out of consciousness on the train. How the hell was I even still awake?

It had *literally* been days since I last slept, *plural*. DAYS.

I stumbled to my bed and was out like a light.

A few hours later, I awoke to the sound of my alarm. The bags under my eyes were so massive I would definitely be forced to check them in at the airport, but I was determined to make the most of my time in this bucket list destination. There was no way I was going to waste another second in bed, so that nap had to suffice. I showered, put on clothes and was out the door by 9am.

Every corner I turned made me realize just why the city is so widely admired. The beautiful architecture, rich history, colorful gardens and food culture were richer than anything anyone ever communicated to me during a conversation or through a photo. After wandering around the city all day, climbing the stairs of the Eiffel Tower and visiting the Louvre, every last energy source in my body was depleted. My phone already tracked my total walking distance at over ten miles for the day. As the sun set, I purchased a steamy roasted chicken from a street vendor and snacked on it while I walked in the direction of my hostel. I had to be at the airport early the next morning and didn't want to be lost and alone in the dark in Paris with a dead phone and a flight to catch.

As I inhaled my mouthwatering dinner and strolled past dozens of cute little French shops, my phone buzzed. Teodoro finished his shift and wondered what my plans were for the rest of the evening. When I told him I hadn't made any, he took the opportunity to change that.

"I'll meet you at your hostel in an hour. Wear shoes you can walk in." I picked up the pace so I would have time to prepare my luggage for my flight the next morning. Where was he going to take me? Something was telling me I might not have a chance to pack later so I needed to make sure I was prepared for anything. With the twenty minutes of time I had to spare, I went down to the bar and ordered a beer to sip on while I chatted with the bartender.

Right on time, Teodoro appeared and joined me at the bar before inviting me to his place. I knew better, but based on the conversation that we shared the night prior in the dark, I concluded that he was not dangerous, and I was right; he wasn't. My judgement of strangers improved vastly over the years, but my concern in visiting his home was that I knew he wanted to have sex with me, something I was not interested in doing. In order for me to accept his offer to join him, he had to know that I did not want to hook up, nor was I interested in pursuing anything. Had I been intoxicated already, the night may have played out much differently, but we were both sober.

"I would love to join you, but I want to make sure we are on the same page. I only say this because I do not want to lead you on. I am not interested in having sex."

"I promise I'm not trying to pressure you into this, I really want to show you something."

It was his penis.*
(*kidding)

His offer was so mysterious I could not refuse.

We finished our drink at the hostel and embarked on a lovely stroll through the city. Teodoro and I reached a dark and sketchy alley in an area I certainly wouldn't want to be lost in at any hour; even he admitted the neighborhood wasn't great. The dark never bothered me; I've always been a creature of the night.

"This one." He pointed to a beautiful, old gothic building in the middle of the block. I trusted Teodoro—he was open, honest, and respectful since the moment I met him. Even when we were dancing at the club the night before, he didn't put his hands anywhere inappropriate or try kissing me. He kept blowing me away with the way he was treating me. Why didn't I want to get involved with him?

He typed in the code to access the building and inside we went. The hallway was pitch black and he offered to hold my hand so he could guide me through the dark (the building was so old, the hallways were not equipped with lights). Up the stairs we went—all the way to the top floor. He unlocked the door and fumbled around for the light switch.

Blankets and dozens of empty bottles of liquor and wine were strewn about the cozy studio apartment. There was no doubt in my mind that I wasn't the first girl he brought here, and I guarantee I was not the last.

"I promise, this isn't why I brought you here."

Teodoro handed me a fuzzy wine-colored blanket and poured us both a glass, then opened the window above the kitchen sink and climbed through it.

"Come on, take my hand."

Sigh. So Aladdin.

Once I stopped salivating, I passed him the wine and followed him out the window and over a peak on the roof until we reached a flat area at the very top. That was when I realized this was what he wanted to show me, a view that took my breath away a million times over—

Paris from the rooftop.

Never in a million years would I have thought I would be sitting on the roof of a beautiful old gothic building overlooking the entire city of Paris twinkling in lights under the black sky. I was having a hard time determining if this was reality or if I was going to wake up in a hospital after somehow overdosing on alcohol at Oktoberfest. I could see the Eiffel Tower, Arc de Triomphe and so many other things I don't know what to call. I was at a complete loss of words. It was one of the most spectacular views I had ever seen, and it was all because of the kindness of a stranger, trust and some good, old-fashioned honesty.

Our conversation under the stars ran on until far later than I should have allowed—I had to be at the airport in less than four hours and the clock was ticking. Teodoro offered to walk me back to my hostel but I declined and ordered a car. He kissed me on the cheek and held me in his arms for a few moments until my ride pulled up. We never saw each other again, but I will never forget him. He reminded me to trust the universe.

LESSON #20
Honesty is the only policy.

Honesty goes a hell of a lot further than you might think; take it from me. I learned how to lie at a very young age to survive the climate I was in. I was constantly in trouble, always getting yelled at, singled out, told I couldn't do things and so on. If I ever wanted to do something, the answer was always no, so I learned I had to find a more creative way to do it if I really wanted it. Lying was an effective tool and because of it I hurt a lot of people, including myself. Nothing good ever comes from lying. I thought Teodoro would retract his offer if I told him I wasn't interested in sex, but contrary to my belief, the honesty was well-received. I had good intentions and trusted that his were aligned with my own. No one knows what our boundaries are unless we are honest and up front about them.

Had the circumstances been different or if I wasn't emotionally invested in York and sexually involved with so many other people I cared about, Teodoro and I would probably go all the way that night and I would definitely miss my flight the following morning. I suppose this was the Disney version of that—making out (with lots of touching) on a rooftop in Paris. Because I communicated my intentions from the start, I was able to enjoy a one-of-a-kind experience without feeling guilty. I was beginning to observe patterns in the way my relationships were developing.

Fatefully, I was still alone, still blindly searching for my "soulmate." My childhood dream of being swept off my feet by a foreigner had still not come to fruition, nor had any of my other fantasies, but would they ever? Am I doomed to be eternally single? What if I was surrounded by love all along, yet misidentified it for something else?

All of these questions, still no answers.

Time and time again, honesty achieved a positive outcome, yet I was still exerting tons of effort performing maintenance on my dishonesty to myself.

*

TWENTY-ONE

ULRIC

"Replace fear of the unknown with curiosity."
Unknown

Despite the high in Paris, the loneliness was excruciating. I never thought I was going to get married or have a family of my own one day. Love terrified me. I was finally learning how to connect with people, but I routinely set dynamite under the bridges and gave us both remotes so we could decimate our progress at any time. The resulting destruction stung less and less and now I was numb to both the highs and the lows. I longed for emotional connection more than anything else.

I craved intimacy.

I struggled to make genuine connections with anyone for years; it was either have sex or be platonic, and almost every guy chose sex (duh). Chasing me was like a dog chasing its tail. At this point, all anyone needed to do to have sex with me was be attractive and talk to me long enough to make it through a few drinks. I was that easy. Many single women are.

***

My flight into Edinburgh was delayed by almost a full day due to a wicked storm, but I eventually made it safe and sound. It was hours after dark and my only option was to hop on the last double-decker bus of the night and head to the city center. I walked two miles in the darkness surrounded by falling snowflakes, praying to Steve Jobs that my iPhone wouldn't breathe its dying breath before I reached my hostel with the dwindling 4%... 3% battery life it was hanging on by.

Twenty minutes later I saw the sign glowing in the distance; I looked down at my phone and in that moment it flatlined. After checking in, I wandered up to my room to drop off my things and nurse my phone back to life, then ventured to the lounge area with one of my dorm-mates. I spent the first half of the day waiting for my delayed flight to board in the Reykjavik airport. A dozen other tipsy travelers were enjoying the snowy evening in the company of wonderful strangers and pints of beer fresh from the Scottish taps.

Not even five minutes passed before I was setting up a supersized version of Jenga with three Germans and an Amsterdam local. The hostel community is one of the most open and friendly in the world. Everyone appears to know each other, yet know nothing about each other at all. We are bound together by our love of adventure, passion for storytelling, curious demeanors, and mutual trust in the universe. Strangers are just friends you haven't connected with yet.

In the corner of my eye, an attractive man took a seat at a table on the other side of the room. As I took my next turn, I could feel a set of eyes on me. I looked again in the direction of the stranger. Was he staring?

He smiled, stood up, and made his way over to our table, sat beside me, and introduced himself. He, too, had arrived much later than he was originally scheduled due to weather delays, and rather than tell us about himself, the Germans were having fun taking guesses as to where this guy was from based on his accent. It is fascinating how many different accents and languages there are throughout Europe alone. Ten minutes later, the six of us were discussing our outlooks on the world. When the bar announced it was closing for the night, everyone in the group connected on social media and went their separate ways. I didn't expect to see any of them again, but Ulric dropped a comment about grabbing breakfast in the morning so I figured, *why not?*

"Shoot me a message," slipped out of my mouth as I scampered off to bed.

***

Hey! Any plans for the day?

I rolled over on my bunk bed to a message from the cute foreign guy I met in the common area the night before. I gazed out the window to see the entire street blanketed in the most beautiful dusting of snow. My original plan for the day was now shattered due to the snowflakes still trickling from above, but to be honest, I was in heaven.

Not only had the hostel cancelled their walking tour, but nearly everything else in the city was closed. Local transportation was limited. The castle and museums did not open. The streets were completely still. My only choice was to get outside and explore it by foot through the wind and snow... Perhaps I'd find a quaint café to sit down in with a coffee and write, just like J.K. Rowling apparently used to do while writing *Harry Potter*. [Ironically, this is the exact city I started journaling; which is what evolved into the book you are reading right now. Be prepared for an excerpt.]

What can I say? Scotland inspired me.

It was hours before noon and there were so many things I wanted to accomplish, but was confined to the radius of wherever I was willing to walk. Ulric and I connected in the lobby to request breakfast recommendations from a local Scotsman... and naturally we ended up at a pub. (Of course.) We made our way towards the recommended bar and sat near the window with a view of the beautiful white streets outside, continuing our conversation from the night before over our breakfast. One hour turned into three. Our lattes were soon replaced by beer. A couple more hours went by and before we realized it, it was dark outside and we still hadn't budged—we were *still* sitting at the same table when the street lights came on.

We spent the majority of our time in Scotland exploring not the beautiful city around us, but each other's minds. We talked about times our hearts were broken, what home is like, and what the future held. We were focused solely on each other. No topic was untouchable. His mind was as spongey as my own; filled with a plethora of scientific, philosophical, memorized and calculated knowledge that had every cell in my prefrontal cortex illuminated like the Eiffel Tower. We ended up staying the night together and the following morning I actually did miss my connecting flight.

We didn't *need* to sleep together, but after drinking all day we *chose* to. Did we have a genuine connection? How do you know if you've made one? Is there a specific point in time? Will you know it happens as soon as it happens? How can we be certain another person has the same thoughts or feels the same way?

Simple. Talk about it by expressing your own.

Ulric and I both came to the city with a list of things to accomplish but did none of them because of what was outside our control—the weather. We didn't have to spend our entire day together, we both wanted to because our options were limited and the conversation was fun, honest, and thought-provoking. Time is the most valuable thing we all have, and we almost shared an entire weekend of our time with each other. If we enjoyed a couple days together, why not a lifetime?

We talked some more over our coffees and croissants the following morning before his train was scheduled for departure. I walked with him to the station and waved him off as he boarded, but I already knew nothing would come of this. Many things test our emotional limits and what we think is possible and long distance is one of them. Back when I was with Ben, I would cry if he went out of town for a few days simply because I was lonely. That is an unhealthy reason to cry; I was dependent upon his presence for my happiness. Because of this, I thought long-distance relationships were impossible.

Again and again, I thought I met the love of my life and messed everything up. Ulric helped me see that connection is possible with literally anyone in the world so long as both individuals want to connect with each other in the first place. We were born on the opposite side of the globe in two completely different realities, but were still able to relate in many ways. We were both infected with the most ruthless illness in the universe—

Curiosity.

The only medicine for curiosity is exploration.

Snow wasn't enough to prevent either of us from exploring; it was merely the subject of our exploration that we adapted to the circumstances. Maybe Ulric was the foreign boy I always dreamed of; the one I craved since childhood that would make me the star of my own Lizzie McGuire Movie. All I needed was a stage to sing on.

Upon returning home, we stayed in contact for a few weeks but it was short-lived because I was addicted to work, scared of love and commitment, had no idea how to communicate my emotions, nor did I believe I was capable of a long distance relationship, otherwise I would already want to be in one with York. I was convinced there was an expiration date because everything else did. Why was I looking at the end before we even said goodbye?

LESSON #21
Fear results in self-sabotage.

Why was I so afraid of love, anyway? It's obvious to me now since I never understood it and I always got hurt from loving when I was younger. I didn't even realize how many situations I experienced up to this point which led me to believe love was something that it wasn't. It always felt like it was my fault my relationships didn't work but I was never able to understand why, so I just kept running and accepted that something was wrong with me and there was nothing I could do about it.

It was on the plane home from Scotland that I started writing what evolved into this "chapter," though at the time it was really more of a wine-drunk rant about my hopelessness of finding love in my notebook. While I successfully managed to quit cigarettes at this point in my life, my drinking problem still had its moments.

Here's a little excerpt—

"It doesn't make sense to me
How could you have such a short cameo in my life
Yet still established this much connection?
Hopefully I wake up tomorrow with no memory of you.
I don't want to continue searching for 'you'
Knowing that you are unattainable.
Is there a way for me to move forward?
Please, show me."

This could literally apply to anyone I was involved with. Here I was again, walking through a door before closing the last. The lines became so blurred over the years I didn't know what I was doing anymore.

I can't stress this enough—this is <u>only</u> a stress when seeing multiple people simultaneously; *the result of neglecting to close doors before opening new ones.* This was perhaps one of my worst habits—one I *promised* myself I would not do a long time ago. Ironically, Zachariah, the next person I got involved with upon returning from this trip flipped my love life upside-down, but I was pretty much in love with York without really realizing just how strongly I felt about him. I had so many doors open, there was no chance I would ever be able to make a commitment with Ulric or any one person. Having numerous doors to choose from decreases the probability of walking through the right one. Every door is a distraction. If you want to be with a person, there are no other doors!

At one point Ulric volunteered to fly across the globe just to see me, but there was no way I could allow him to do that. He will end up with a great woman one day, but I know he's not my person. I cared about him and wanted to remove myself from his life before I wasted more of it. I didn't trust myself with his heart because I didn't trust myself with mine. The one and only thing all my failed relationships had in common was this: <u>ME</u>. And I knew it. It was why I took myself off the apps and stopped seeking new people to date the year prior. How many times was I going to make decisions from a place of low frequency and continue to sabotage the positive opportunities that existed in my life? Fear results in a reaction instead of a response.

In modern society, people are together because they choose to be. Freedom of choice is a huge responsibility. Choices are merely distractions because when we compare things, we focus more on the difference between the things rather than the thing we truly want. We will chase forever if we fail to understand this truth.

Imagine I have a key in one hand and nothing in the other. If I ask you to choose a hand, there is a fifty percent chance you will select the one with the key. On the contrary, if I had ten cups on the table and put that same key under one of those cups, you would only have a ten percent chance of picking the right one. Which odds would you rather have? Now more than ever, we have too many options when it comes to dating and love. Online dating is a numbers game: the more you play, the more you lose. The question is, *what are you playing for?*

***

Enough about strangers! Everyone starts off as a stranger at some point in our lives and there are plenty of other amazing ones I cannot write about since there are simply not enough letters in the alphabet. I'm sure your attention span isn't quite that extensive either. Mine isn't.

It's time I tell you about men who were *more* than just strangers to me; the ones I really got to know and love, the ones who taught me more about myself, life and the universe than I ever expected to learn. I want to share with you how I permitted my distorted idea of love shaped by my past relationships to prevent healthy, new ones from flourishing. At the time of these interactions, I wasn't able to see it because I never considered how my past pain was influencing my present. I was blind to my own self-sabotaging behaviors.

I've said it once and I'll say it again: men and women want the same thing. We all want to feel loved, appreciated, safe, seen, heard and happy. We all want to be with someone whom does not judge us by our past and wants to be part of our future without an alternate agenda. We must each be independently content by ourselves, and want to be with each other because we are in agreement that life is better that way. We all seek love that is unconditional, meaningful, and long-lasting. We all want to be with someone who wants us as much as we want them.

It is the adventure of how we find this "love" that makes all the difference. But the how is rooted in the now, and I still had no control over my emotions, urges, addictions or anything else for that matter; meaning I was failing to take ownership of or control over my own actions and thus incapable of change.

Prepare to be confused, because after promising myself I wouldn't overlap the people I was dating, I ended up overlapping half a dozen of them.

I was living out a real life version of *The Bachelorette*.

*

Part III
Love Limbo

TWENTY-TWO

VANCE

"One ought to hold on to one's heart; for if one lets it go,
one soon loses control of the head too."
Friedrich Nietzsche

People claim that "first impressions are everything," and they kinda are. First dates are a fantastic indicator of what a relationship with someone might look like. The night we met was a couple weeks after the traumatic morning I witnessed Noah swiping around on his dating app while I was still naked in bed. I just wanted to feel wanted.

Enter, Vance.

His initial lengthy personalized message caught my attention. He was a curiously brilliant mind with a spontaneity that matched that of my own; even our match percentage on the dating site was close to 100% (though I shared 90-100% matches with so many men even that eventually lost its buzz). We bantered through the app for a few days; he was witty, smart, and funny. The stereotypical dating boxes were checked except a few, which is to be expected.

Our unique story started at a bar, and it is a first date neither one of us will ever be able to forget, even if we wanted to.

Part A – The Attention Getter
First impressions are artistic expressions. It is the audio and visual
we give people the first time they see us combined with the feeling
they have in our presence.

I recognized him right away. He looked sharp in his office attire and was more attractive in person than his photos. The collar of his button-up shirt was crisp and even his shoes were squeaky clean. I was still in my work clothes, too, yet for the first time in my extensive history of first dates, I was the one feeling underdressed.

He complimented me and said something cute, we hugged and the conversation flowed pretty naturally from there. We had so much to talk about, we covered everything from local sports teams, families, politics, philosophy, TV shows, conspiracy theories and more. He was clever and creative and everything he said had my head spinning around in thought. He made me think. He had so much to say.

Who knows how many drinks we had; I was too entangled in our conversation to count but there were quite a few. Like Ivan, he ordered the next round before finishing the current one. He was enjoying the evening just as much as I was—so much so, that we decided we weren't ready for it to end when the bar told us it was closing. We decided to get some food to add to all the alcohol we were holding in our stomachs.

"I want to take you to this little place by the beach." He said.

We hopped in his car and embarked on an adventure.

***

Upon walking into the restaurant, we were devastated to learn they closed their kitchen just moments prior, so we did what anyone who just walked into a bar would do—we ordered a round of drinks. The more we talked, the more we drank. Drinking with this guy was fun and I was getting pretty tipsy.

We quickly downed our beers and rush ordered *another* round before the bar closed. Would I make it to work the next morning? I didn't even care. I was so drunk that I was convinced Vance was my soulmate, sacrificing a sick day wouldn't hurt. We poured back the final sips of our beer.

"No more for meeee!" I slurred, completely sloshed on a weeknight. We closed down our second bar together and walked back to the car. According to the clock, it was already tomorrow.

"Want to sit on the beach for a little bit? I know this really great spot up the road."

We were both in our irresponsible primes.

"That sounds awesome. Let's go." I replied.

Part B – The Bond
Connections are made when people share the same emotion and physical feeling simultaneously. We bond with each other when creating a genuine memory.

We hopped back in his car (I cannot believe he drove) and headed up the PCH towards Malibu. The reflection of the moon shimmering above the black ocean waves was mesmerizing. I was completely focused on the beauty of the world around me and the sound of Vance's voice ricocheting through my ear canals, though I was too intoxicated by this point to comprehend much of what he was actually saying. I never imagined I'd be drunk in the untimely hours of the morning sitting shotgun next to an un-vetted stranger I met on the internet. Surely, this was a recipe for disaster and my body would be found off the coast tomorrow morning and my parents would hear their worst nightmare live on the news.

Vance found a parking spot near a pile of rocks and we got out and climbed down into a tiny cove. We made out for a few minutes before he abruptly asked me, "Have you ever gone skinny dipping in the ocean?"

At that point in time, I had not.

It was the middle of February, the water was as cold as ice and we did not fully realize what we were getting ourselves into. The moon was so bright we needed nothing else to guide us. We were in no way prepared for any of what we were about to do. Waves were crashing against the rocks, spraying us in a mist that would surely freeze us to death, but we just went for it. It wasn't every day I met someone as wild and adventurous as myself. While I remember this night to be pretty epic, the mere seconds I spent naked with Vance in the Pacific Ocean were excruciatingly painful and far from "sexy." I felt my entire body convulsing as the waves pricked my skin like a million needles with each crash.

After a few minutes, we were pretty much in agreement—

"LET'S GET THE F*** OUT OF HERE!"

This whole thing was an absolutely brilliant bad idea. We took off towards the shore and dried off as much as we could before cramming our wet, shivering bodies back into our now damp clothes. Granules of sand were stuck in every crease of my skin. We climbed back up the rocks and into his car where we blasted the heater and butt-warmers until it felt like a sauna, complete with condensation on the windows.

Holy hell, what a wild first date.

Remember the whole reason we were *still* out in the first place? For food? The night still wasn't over. We got pretty sidetracked...

Part C – The Chase
Everything that leads up to the first time having sex.

It was well after midnight and we had yet to eat anything, but a food truck is always open somewhere in Los Angeles. We grabbed a few tacos, but then he wanted to come inside my apartment to eat them (much like Martin). Since my roommates were home, I let him in but immediately he made a sexual advance on me—he completely skipped the tacos. I was triggered. I told him I was not ready for that and asked him to leave but he persisted to push for it (which was likely due to the level of intoxication he was feeling and the mixed signals I was sending him). He tried to convince me that I wanted it, too, but I did not.

After a few unsuccessful attempts to sway my decision, he finally left. I saw him a few times after that under different circumstances, one of which we did *some* dirty things, but I still didn't want to have sex with him. He drowned me in his ocean of attention—texting me, calling me, and ruthlessly asking me to make plans. No matter how many times I said "no," he would not stop unless I didn't respond. Eventually I lost my patience and ghosted him. He was sweet, but I was simply not interested.

I didn't know how to explain why I didn't want to have sex with him. Something felt off, but I had no idea what that meant or why I felt that way. I enjoyed his drunken company but in my sobriety felt overwhelmed. It was like a barrier I didn't want to cross no matter how drunk I was and I could never figure out why, so I ran; usually back to bed with Lyle.

Our time together always ended with some of the longest drunk kisses I remember. He read the signals I was giving, as I did his. *This* is what determines who is a good kisser, and almost all the guys in this book were "good kissers" in my opinion. There is no "perfect method" or formula or movement for kissing, nor is there for sex. Everything is a matter of chemistry and connection. It is all natural. If you want another person to consider you to be a "good kisser" or "good in bed," follow their lead, ask and be receptive to their desires without judgement, and respond to what you perceive. LISTEN. Be observant. If you don't know, ask! Good kissing and good sex are about connecting with the person you are with and enjoying yourselves—nothing else. It's that simple. It is not necessarily recreating the craziest move you saw in a porn that one time or even reaching climax.

Ever wonder why you can't get someone out of your head after kissing them? After you feel that rush of dopamine? Oxytocin? Serotonin? We don't have to be "in love" to feel the sensation that kissing or even something as modest as touching naturally delivers. Sex? Can you imagine how much weight that holds on our bodies?!

Chemistry can't be forced, you either have it or you don't. When I was drinking with Vance I felt it, but when I was sober, it was missing. I cared for Vance but failed to share my intentions with him early on. When we first met, I wasn't the type of girl to sleep around—Lyle got to bypass all my filters because of the agreement we put in place, but the rest of my standards slowly started to crumble from there.

At the end of every visit, I would part ways knowing in the back of my mind I would see him again, but unsure when that would be. I thought I might have a future with him, but every time we reconnected I was reminded why we didn't, nothing ever changed. We would talk and drink a lot, then just end up making out until he made a sexual advance. This cycle of shenanigans became welcome in both our lives for several years.

***

How's my favorite person doing?

There it was—his routine, semi-annual message.

We made plans later that week for food and drinks. When the evening finally arrived, he asked if it was cool if one of his buddies joined us. I met a couple people from his life years prior, but meeting a friend tonight was unusual. He assured me it was no big deal. But was it? *What was I doing?*

Dinner and drinks went by fast. The boys were laughing and having a blast when I showed up and even the waitress was enjoying herself because by the end of the night, she had practically joined us at the table. At some point, the buddy's girlfriend arrived and what was originally supposed to be the two of us evolved into a double date I never signed up for. Eventually we migrated from the restaurant to a nearby bar. What type of shenanigans was this night going to bring?

We ordered our first round of drinks and found a nice table to stand at beneath a heat lamp. His friends started asking questions about how we met and we shared a considerably shorter version of the first date story you just finished reading. It was getting late and I knew I needed to get out of there before I drank too much. I had to break the cycle—I wanted the drunken make-out sessions with him to stop. After two drinks, I said my goodbyes and darted out to my car. It was before midnight, and probably the earliest I ever escaped from a night out with Vance .

Several blocks into my trek home, I started to notice the vehicle behind me was making all the same turns, placing me on immediate alert. *Was I being followed?* I took a detour, but again, the car continued to shadow my every move. Eventually I sped through a light and lost them, but I parked behind my apartment building to be safe and ran inside through the alleyway.

Phew, I made it.

Just when I thought I was clear, my phone started buzzing.

> *Hey you, I'm outside your door.*
> *Would it be too much if I asked to come in?*

I peeked out the window and held my breath. There he was, standing on the other side. What made him think he could show up here? Was there some sort of miscommunication?

He told me he *thought* it was what I wanted; which means I steered him very wrong. Early on we had a conversation in which I mentioned women like to be pursued, but this was not how I intended it. Following someone home is not acceptable.

Some might be flattered a love interest would show up at their door unannounced, others might feel unsafe and contemplate calling the police. I, on the other hand, was triggered, yet chose to respond anyways. I grabbed my phone and keys and wedged myself out my front door without letting him in the same way you would go out the door so your new puppy doesn't squeeze by and dart out into the street. There is no other reason to show up intoxicated at someone's house that late at night other than sex. As a precautionary measure, I locked the door from the inside on my way out so he couldn't try to go in (which he tried to do). His behavior was too predictable. I was frustrated and just wanted to go to sleep, but I continued to entertain it as a possibility because a part of me liked the attention (this is why girls make out with guys at bars and it never goes anywhere). I made out with him again and when I asked him to leave, he told me he loved me.

This was not the only time he said it but I couldn't say it back because I did not feel the same way. In the majority of my early relationships I said those three powerful words to only a few people and considering those relationships all failed, I struggled to say it to anyone else for years. I wanted to know with 100% certainty that I could commit to someone before using those three powerful words again.

I thought I might love him but something always felt off. I wasn't quite sure what it was. I thought the infrequency of the time we spent together and the fact that we never had sex made it impossible for love to grow, but I was wrong; that was _why_ it happened. Love made no sense to me.

LESSON #22
There are no boundaries until boundaries are established.

And as you can see, neither one of us ever set any!

Boundaries are a two way street and we were naked on the first night. From our very first date, we literally crossed all the boundaries—personal, societal, legal probably, and who knows what else. It makes complete sense why he would think following me home might be acceptable, I led him on and I never told him anything was unacceptable. I never told him why I didn't want to have sex with him, I just kept leading him on, then pushing him away because he did something that triggered me. He knew I was sleeping with other people and still kept trying, I even told him of Lyle's existence on several occasions so he was well aware I was having sex with other people and never him. Why didn't I want to have sex with Vance if I enjoyed sex so much?

Knowing *how* he loved me, having sex would be a disservice to us both. I had to be sober to understand there was a *moral* barrier. Our relationship was unhealthy because neither one of us knew how to establish boundaries—the real problem. He continued reaching out for years and because I felt connected to him, I felt obligated to respond. I knew he wasn't the right person for me and vice versa, so why was I still entertaining the idea?

***

Okay so remember when I told you a few chapters ago there was a time gap while I was in college from Simon to Teodoro? The next two chapters are about to fill that in.

*

TWENTY-THREE

WILLIAM

"If you find yourself in a hole, stop digging."
Will Rogers

Summer was coming to a close and for the next year and a half, I would be spending approximately all of my time indoors, *BUT* I was also excited because this would be the final eighteen months of hell after *years* of not committing to a major. I prolonged my graduation with my own indecisiveness. For someone who hated school so much, I spent an awful lot of time in it.

If I was ever going to graduate I knew I had to focus on one thing and one thing alone—SCHOOL. It had to be my number one priority (after my job), which meant the best thing I had to offer anyone for dating's sake was my third priority. Dating was my biggest distraction aside from all the drugs I was doing. Intoxication was the only reality I was able to enjoy so I learned how to manage it while living a highly functional life; the absolute worst kind of addiction. Not only had I deceived everyone around me, but I deceived myself.

I never really took my education seriously because I hated school—I still think college is a waste of money. I got hired at my first nine-to-five without a degree as an accounting clerk. I changed my major from Mathematics to Civil Engineering to Business before I finally graduated. Having a degree is worth a few additional years of pain and suffering... right? That's what we are all led to believe, at least. But for what? Crippling debt and a job that is not fulfilling? Anything they teach you in college can be learned without going.

After the failed two years of online dating and my experimental one night-stand phase ending with Simon, I deleted every dating account I had. No more swiping. No more sleeping around. It was time to put on my big girl pants and evolve into a responsible adult, but there was one last thing I needed to do before closing out the summer...

Party one last time, of course.

My final weekend of summer break was just over twenty-four hours from completion and I was determined to make the most of it. It was also my friend Wilma's last weekend before she started her next degree, so she was equally excited to go out. We had been going pretty crazy over recent months.

We walked up to the bar and ordered our first drink before finding an open area to stand in. After chatting with a few strangers and quickly sipping our glasses empty, Wilma and I found ourselves ready for another round and made our way back to the bar. Just as I was about to wedge myself into a small gap that opened up in the sea of people, some guy squeezed in front of me and reached his arm over the kid standing in front of him, immediately got the bartender's attention and ordered.

"How'd you do that?!" I asked in astonishment.

He turned around.

"Oh, I'm so sorry... Did I cut you? What are you having? Let me get your drink. I'm William." He said with a smile.

Damn that was smooth.

Wilma disappeared into the swarm of men buzzing behind me, so I decided to stick around to figure out who the heck this guy was. Our brief conversation proved we had a few things in common, and I found him pretty attractive, too. They say you find what you're looking for when you stop looking. Would that be the case here?

Abruptly, my friend emerged from the crowd.

"We need to leave."

"What happened? Is everything okay?"

She gave me no further explanation and I wrapped up my chat with William. "Thanks so much for my drink, it was nice to meet you."

"You, too."

Wilma and I walked towards the exit.

"He was cute! Are you going to see him again?"

"He didn't take my number."

She didn't miss a beat—she clutched my arm and dragged me right back to William. "Ask for her number." She ordered.

Damn, killer wingman.

He took my info and we went our separate ways. I thought for sure I would never hear from this guy again; I assumed he only took my digits because he was held at a socially metaphorical gunpoint.

The next morning, I woke up to a message—

> *Hey. It was really great meeting you last night.*
> *Let's play tennis sometime* ☺

I smiled and contemplated whether or not and how I would respond, and whether or not I wanted to get my butt kicked by this guy. I hadn't touched a racket in years and I was not really in a place for dating considering I was about to start the school session. Alas, only a few messages were exchanged before we had plans to get together later that week. What are the chances that as soon as I hit the pause button on dating, I meet a promising suitor at a bar I frequented almost every weekend?

Our first date was at a popular local wine bar. Upon paying the bill, he walked me to my car, kissed me on the cheek and waved me off. I was as smitten as the heart-eyed emoji. William was cute and polite and exhibited that he was respectful and interested. To top it off, I had more in common with him than I had with anyone all summer. (Although most of those guys were one night stands...)

We found ourselves on the tennis court the following weekend which was a complete and utter dumpster fire. I partied *way* too hard the night before despite promising myself I would put that lifestyle behind me to focus on school. Somehow I still managed to drag my hungover self out of bed to play tennis, of all things, early on a Saturday morning with William.

Every time I caught a glimpse of direct sunlight, I felt like I was going to collapse on the ground, or projectile vomit, or both. It was cruel and unusual punishment for my dehydrated, weak and poisoned body, but my body was going to have to figure out how to endure this discomfort at any cost because William might be my "soulmate."

As you might imagine, I could hardly keep a rally going but despite my struggle, he made losing fun because we weren't really keeping score. We grabbed breakfast after the disaster, but the longer I stared into the hole of my bagel, the more nauseated I became and the more I wished it was the hole of a toilet bowl or trash bin. I was past the point of no return and had to get home to lay down in fetal position before I gave birth to the gin and beer byproduct of the night before. I rushed back to my car and managed to make it back to my apartment before the wrath of the hangover hit its peak. I apologized and presumed I had just blown any chance I might have with him, because if that didn't do it, the upcoming chunks would certainly solidify that.

Later that afternoon, my phone awoke me from my snooze.

I had a blast with you this morning,
let's try again another time when you're feeling better.

I didn't ruin a thing.

***

Months went by and despite the fact that little in life ever goes according to plan, we were *still* going on regular adventures. Work kept him later than expected? We'd reschedule. Traveling abroad? We called and video chatted. I had a huge final coming up?

He waited a few extra days to see me. Date planning? We would try something new together. Sex? It happened when it happened, and I even stopped collab-ing with Lyle. Car broke down at 2am? We waited for a tow truck and told stories outside in the cold.

We were both along for the ride, whatever that was, with no urgency to reach any destination whatsoever. Neither of us knew, we never really talked about the future, but I was thinking it might be, like, *forever*. I even introduced him to my friends and vice versa. For the first time in a long time, I felt like this was love *for real*. Months of getting to know William gave me a pretty good idea of who he was and what his values were, but I was too anxious about the future to have a conversation about it and he never brought it up, either. We couldn't be bothered, we were just enjoying things as they were.

Unfortunately the more time I spent with William, the less time I spent on my schoolwork. Regular sleepovers resulted in late mornings at the office; and it got so bad my boss actually had to say something to me about it for the first time since I was involved with York. I was working overtime, juggling a full-time course load, and just when I didn't think things could get any worse, that was when I got the Chlamydia news from the doctor.

Everything in my life was catching fire. My motto was "*you can sleep when you're dead,*" and I was sleeping about 3-5 hours per night. Maybe it is when we reach the point of choosing not to sleep that we become the living dead, for there is no longer any shift in our consciousness. I was trying to cram so many things into my schedule, some days I even forgot to eat. I was on the express train of my own mortality and totally fine with it because I thought I would suddenly be happy after the train reached the station and I completed my degree.

Attempting to squeeze William in any time slot I possibly could was growing more stressful every day and when I did see him, I wasn't emotionally or mentally there. I was losing my mind between school and work by smoking, drinking, snorting or popping something at any given opportunity just to make it all disappear. I was doing everything else because I thought or felt like I had to, not because I wanted to. I wanted to spend time with William, but I had to get a degree because my parents wanted me to have it and I had to go to work because I wanted to be independent of them. Bills don't pay themselves; I was convinced my degree would be my ticket to freedom.

Gradually, William grew distant. The time we were spending together was stripped of exciting adventures and replaced with TV show marathons or drinking to forget about all the other things that were stressing us out. He stopped initiating sex with me. We were together in physical location, yet emotionally isolated. We were hardly even talking anymore. What happened? Could I fix this?

We previously discussed spending New Year's together, but a few weeks before that was when I got the news about having Chlamydia (and I informed him immediately). Shortly before midnight he told me he was going to be in one place, then shared his geolocation with me which showed him to be somewhere completely different. When midnight arrived… radio silence. He didn't wish me a "Happy New Year" until the following morning, though I didn't wish him one until he wished me one first. It was one of the most devastating nights of my life. It was the night I had to accept William moved on and was merely my memory now.

We saw each other a couple times after that but he was already emotionally somewhere else. He was soon tagged in photos with another girl on social media. I felt betrayed and hurt he was happy with someone who wasn't me. My coping mechanism was to go get inebriated.

I buried my head in my textbooks and drowned out all thoughts of him with various drugs because it hurt too much to remain sober. My efforts to fill the void were taking a disastrous toll on every aspect of my life, especially my friendships. This was the point at which I chose to go off my birth control so I would be less inclined to sleep around and have unprotected sex. (This strategy actually worked for me.)

It was easier for me to continue to numb myself rather than stare myself in the face and acknowledge that I had more issues than I knew how to handle. My attention was always somewhere else *and* I was always under the influence. Additionally, I believed that being in a relationship meant you had to have sex with that person, so when he didn't try to do it, I thought that meant he wasn't into me anymore.

Eventually (now), I see that William didn't necessarily distance himself; I distanced myself from him *first* due to the demands of college and work, but neglected to view it from that perspective. I took William's detachment personally instead of realizing I had a lot of unaddressed trauma. I never wanted to push him away, but given the circumstances, he would be foolish to stay and wait for me to love him the way he deserved.

The next time our paths crossed was about two years later.

***

After I graduated, I suddenly had more hours than I knew what to do with. I downloaded a different dating app to put myself back on the market. Sure enough, William's profile was one of the first ones that showed up, what are the chances? I remember exiting the app to avoid swiping on him at least twice, but the third time he appeared, I decided I would give it another chance. Would he? I was in a different place and no longer bitter about the way things ended the first time. Sure enough, it was a match!

We picked up right where we left off, but I had very few friends or hobbies because I spent the last year and a half working, going to school, doing drugs and drinking alcohol. It became clear to him that something was different one night when we were out drinking with his buddies at a local bar.

"We're going outside for a smoke, I'll be right back." William mentioned as he handed me his beer. Nothing new, when we first met, this was a pretty common occurrence.

"Can I join?" I asked. *This* was new.

He was stunned. Several weeks prior I failed my first attempt to quit smoking and I was feeling particularly low in the self-esteem department. I managed to hide the habit from him completely for the entire time we initially dated just as I had done with almost every other guy, unless, of course, they were also a smoker.

It was around this time I reconnected with York, who was coming back to my city for a visit. The following day I flew to Europe for a vacation where I hooked up with someone else, *then* went to Paris where I met Teodoro. I was too busy drowning in the attention to notice how shallow the water was. All I had to do was stand up to be above it all. I was having sex for all the wrong reasons and in most situations, failing to even have a conversation about it. I was addicted to feeling *wanted*—that was what satisfied the psychotic fantasy of love I created in my mind.

Needless to say, I didn't hear from William much after I got back from that vacation. My behavior changed because I felt guilty for entertaining a relationship with him knowing I was more interested in York and getting and involved with several others within a one week timespan. I was so ashamed of my own behavior I didn't even want to date new people anymore.

***

For some reason, the universe wanted us to try again.

Why is honestly beyond me. Third time's the charm, eh?

We crossed paths in an airport terminal about a year later, and this time, I was starting to gain control of my life back from my various addictions. I completely stopped smoking cigarettes by that point and was no longer sleeping around as irresponsibly as before, but I was in touch with Lyle, Vance, Xerxes, York, and Zachariah.

After William and I both returned from our separate trips, we hung out a few times. I was honest with William about the cigarettes and told him about my journaling therapy, *and* that I was considering converting it into a book. Little did I know how much work that was going to be... The journaling only took about six months. The editing and *therapy* aspect of this took almost two years and is ongoing even as I type these words.

Nevertheless, I chose not to focus on William because I was newly captivated by Zachariah at the time. Shocking? Not really. At this point, I had clear behavioral patterns and I was probably the only one that didn't recognize that.

LESSON #23
If both people want to make it work, they will.
No matter what.

These are literally his exact words and it's one of the truest truths out there. The future *has* to be a mutual goal, regardless of whatever else life throws into the mix. William and I didn't work because I never made him my priority nor had I achieved a complete and honest understanding as to what, exactly, love was. When I eventually had the time to devote to him, I showed him no loyalty and gave my attention to other people... *Twice*.

No wonder we didn't work, I was too busy playing the field.

Every relationship is the result of two people choosing each other regardless of when or where or what or why or how; no outside circumstance has any weight on what keeps two people together if they want to be with each other.

I chose York and Zachariah over him.

Twice the universe brought William and I back together and *twice* I directed my attention elsewhere instead of really giving us a chance. Because I had not addressed the reason William and I did not work the first time, I always feared he would choose another girl over me when it was me who never made him a priority to begin with. Would I ever put *him* first, no matter what?

I promised myself that I wouldn't date anyone until I was done writing and editing these horrific dating chronicles. I didn't think it was right to for me to continue inflicting wounds on people because *I was running away from love* and *chasing* sex, yet *still,* even after everything that happened thus far, foolishly confusing the two with each other. Because I had not yet realized sex was the method I was using to cope with my loneliness, I was holding on to a false idea of what a relationship looks like.

At the peak of my self-sabotage and self-destruction, I was binging on alcohol, banging strangers, puffing weed, snorting blow, popping whatever pills I could get my hands on and inhaling ciggies like they were oxygen whilst the people who loved me really didn't have any idea what my life was actually like. I was very selective with the information I shared with people and too successful at being a functioning addict for my own good.

WHAT WAS THE VOID I WAS *REALLY* TRYING TO FILL?

We are all trying to fill it, and there are infinite ways to do so. It is the root of <u>all</u> addiction. We fail to realize how many people we impact, both positively and negatively, on our quest to fill it.

I lost control of my love life and was FINALLY beginning to realize that my love life was the exact thing controlling me. I needed to grab it by the horns and tame it before I lost myself in it completely.

*

TWENTY-FOUR

XERXES

"Life is more fun if you play games."
Roald Dahl

Xena and I were drinking at my favorite bar on a sunny summer Sunday and out of nowhere, a stranger's hand extended out from over my shoulder and grabbed the bottle of beer out of my hand. Enter the player who changed my game.

"Oh sorry, I didn't mean to scare you, I just wanted to show you the best way to put the lime in your beer." His deep, smoky voice sent shivers down my spine.

"This isn't my first Corona." I smirked.

This guy looked like a supermodel—I felt like Emma Stone's character in *Crazy Stupid Love* when she first saw Ryan Gosling take his shirt off. I was too drunk to realize I was drooling.

His friend and Xena hit it off, too, so the four of us went back to their apartment. Xerxes managed to pass out from his long day of drinking while we were in the car on the way home. Thankfully for the sake of this chapter, that drunk afternoon was not the only time we saw each other.

Upon reaching their place, I poured Xerxes a glass of water and massaged his head until Xena was ready to go. We giggled about Xerxes and his inability to survive the day, and I was given a huge confidence boost that a man as attractive as him was interested in me in the first place.

The next morning, I had a text message from him apologizing for his state of intoxication and a request to make it up to me at dinner later that week. I smiled as I wrote my reply of acceptance. I wanted to give this guy a chance; I was giving myself a chance, too. Only a few days prior, I made my first attempt to stop smoking cigarettes, and at this point in time, was still successful!

Sober, he was a completely different person, he emphasized it by repeatedly reminding me of it; and I could tell he was really trying. So was I, as I was usually under the influence of something. I was captivated by everything about him; there was a whole lot more to this guy than the one that snatched the beer out of my hand at the bar. We ended up having a little extra fun after the bill was paid but I still didn't want to have sex. Shockingly, that night was the first time in six years I climaxed with someone. SIX!

He started calling me on his way home from work and on my lunch breaks to chat, something I hadn't experienced in a long time. We were getting to know each other, going out for food, hanging out at the beach, and even once attended a concert. He introduced me to a bunch of his friends. It felt like we might be going somewhere.

After we slept with each other a handful of times, things started to change. Not only did he stop texting me "Good morning," but he also stopped calling me on his breaks. He stopped reaching out. Eventually he stopped trying to sleep with me. *What happened?*

Here is a list of reasons people cut contact with people—

1. The other person is bored
2. The other person met someone else
3. The other person was triggered by your behavior
4. The other person is playing games with you
5. You hurt them and didn't apologize
6. You have a sex addiction/the other person feels used
7. You looked at them funny
8. The moon is full
9. Squirrel
10. Literally anything

How do you know which it is?

Assume or ask; and regardless of which one or combination of these things it is, if another person discontinues contact with you, it is an indication that they are not interested in pursuing anything with you at this time; and *potentially, never*. Yes, that is dismal, but that's also just the way it is, and it's not personal. Time is finite. A major problem in dating culture is that when someone feels lonely again, a door left open may result in a person randomly walking back into your life in hopes that you will take them back exactly how they left you last... which presumably was in bed.

After a few weeks with Xerxes, I was reassigned to his late night time slot and last minute cancellations. Instead of ghosting him or waiting for him to complete the bread-crumbing process, I decided I was going to handle things a little differently. I decided I would break the cycle.

> *If you don't have respect for me or my time, I've got better things to do.*
> *It was lovely getting to know you. :-**

He didn't like that much.

The idea came from an online dating coach. (Matthew Hussey. He's great.) For the next ten minutes, my phone was bombarded with apology texts. For the first time in weeks, Xerxes was putting in effort!

For a minute, he was hanging out with me again, but eventually returned to indecisive late-night shenanigans. Was he a jerk I wrongfully gave a second chance to? Was he weighing his options and trying to exploit all of them? Was I only able to add value to his life sexually? I've played games before, was he challenging me in an unwinnable battle? Or was I the idiot doing these exact things all along?

His repeated attempts to delay our hang outs at the last minute or bail altogether brought me great frustration. I tried inviting him over to my place on numerous occasions, but he always declined. It was his place, or no place. Why was he unwilling to meet me in the middle? I attempted a different strategy—another stupid game I found out about on the internet to get his attention— "dot-dot-dotting." It is writing a message and never hitting the send button; so it is essentially just ghosting with added effort. It is dependent on the other person checking the chat screen to see the typing bubble, assuming both people are using iMessage or something similar. I was so desperate to be in a relationship I was brainwashing myself.

You can't play Monopoly or Super Smash without selecting your own character first. You also can't play without someone to play against. It turned out that I was playing in solo mode this whole time. Dot-dot-dotting? Seriously?! How ludicrous! There was no way

I had a chance with *any* guy if that was what I thought might get him to commit to me.

As we drifted apart, all we were doing was having meaningless sex, something that anyone can get from anyone depending the distance they are willing to go for it. I stopped asking Xerxes questions about his life, I stopped listening to what he was saying, I stopped trying to be a girlfriend and he stopped doing nice things for me, too. There are a lot of different ways to say this, "our love languages are just different" or "we're just not right for each other," but the reality is that if both people unconditionally love each other and want to be with each other, they will figure it out. Period.

In the final fling days, I caught a glimpse of a duo of wine glasses set on the corner of the nightstand; and I was not one of the consumers. I didn't care that Lyle was sleeping with other people, but for some reason It bothered me that Xerxes was. Why did I feel so possessive? I pretended none of it bothered me because the sex was good.

Xerxes was a free man, and I a free woman; thus we were both free to do whatever and pleasure whomever whenever we pleased. We became two people smoking, drinking, and having sex. This was when William and I reconnected through the dating app and York visited me from out of town, then I connected with multiple people in Europe, including Teodoro. My love life was pure chaos.

Why would anyone want to play cat-and-mouse games with me when they wear their heart on their sleeve? Why would anyone want to emotionally invest in a person who opens their legs before opening their heart? What did I think I was going to catch? I kept throwing a net filled with gaping holes into the sea expecting fish to get caught and stay in it.

LESSON #24
You can't beat a player because you're only playing yourself.

I mean, honestly, what the heck was I actually trying to accomplish? Did I really think playing games, A MANIPULATIVE APPROACH, was going to lead somewhere positive? We see this stuff in magazines, movies, TV shows, and other stuff, but this is not how to find love and intimacy with someone else. It's all fake. Playing stupid games will only win you stupid prizes.

Dating can be a hard-hitting contact sport jam-packed with action, pain, trauma, lessons, hard work, growth, practice, and so much more. Breaking a heart is nothing like breaking a rib or a leg; but it still takes you out of the game for a while. A major aspect of many sports is learning how to bounce back from injuries. Eventually, you'll return and try to make that game-winning play again. The more we play, the more we win *and* the more we lose.

I always thought that if I didn't give a guy "what he wanted," which according to society is SEX, he would never want to make me his girlfriend. But time and time again, giving a guy "what he wanted" resulted in him dropping off after a few days, weeks or months. So what, exactly, is it that guys want? I felt like I tried everything. I was the only common denominator in all my failed relationships, but I still couldn't understand why. I was so fixated on trying to get the guys I went out with to ask me to be their girlfriend, I was having sex with them hoping it would lead to that— a pattern I started after the situation with Quentin to avoid future guilt.

Xerxes and I both had options and issues. Although I was ultimately frustrated with the ways things unfolded, I am grateful for those nights he shared with me. It was a glimpse of hope that I was again going to find someone with whom I felt comfortable enough to climax with.

***

Xerxes and I reconnected one night about a year later.

He prepared an impressive charcuterie plate, opened a bottle of wine, and we talked for hours and gave each other back-massages. It was almost as though the universe was giving us a second chance. Then, he passed out while we were watching a TV show with the volume on super loud and I assumed he was trying to get rid of me, so I just got up and walked out.

Sex establishes both nothing and everything about a relationship. After I had sex with someone once, I became a different person because I was suddenly dependent on them to fill this "need" I had for sex since I could no longer justify sleeping with Lyle. I was projecting my sex addiction, which stemmed from my corrupt relationship with Edward, onto everyone I "dated."

I completely forgot what intimacy was. Real connections are established through platonic friendship.

There can always be another body; there are millions of them all over this planet. Bodies are merely vessels for our consciousness. We do not choose the flesh we enter this reality in, but we do choose what we do with it.

***

The last time I talked to Xerxes, he reminded me that *I was initially the one who prefaced our encounters by saying that it would be strictly sexual* and that I was the one not looking for anything serious. We met right around the time Lyle expressed interest in dating me and I felt guilty having sex with him because I didn't want him in that way (much like how things were with Vance). I started to preface *all* hook-ups as sex-only situations since I was trying to be honest about my intentions—How did I forget that?!

Turns out I really was just playing games with myself after all. Why was I torturing all these guys?

Why was I torturing myself?

*

TWENTY-FIVE

YORK

"Until you heal the wounds of your past, you are going to bleed."
Iyanla Vanzant

By now, you probably have some idea just how important York is to this story because he's mentioned in almost a dozen chapters. He found me online right after the short-lived fling with Noah and the wild first date with Vance. My roommates and I were marathon watching something on Netflix when my phone buzzed on the table—

> *Looks like I meet the minimum requirements from your profile in the "What I'm looking for" section. Hi, I'm York. It's nice to match you.*

This isn't verbatim, but the message immediately caught my attention. My curiosity was ignited and I felt compelled to explore his dating profile. According to our match percentage, we were only a few points shy of perfect. We were an extraordinarily rare pair and neither one of us claimed to be looking for anything serious from the get-go, but that was only a half-truth on my part. At least he was honest about his intentions.

We met at a bar and talked for a few hours over some beer. I remember smiling the whole time, it felt like we already knew each other and this wasn't the first time we were hanging out. From the moment I first sat down at the table I knew this guy was going to change my life. Almost like that corny, "I knew he/she was the one from the moment we first met." Only, I never thought I was going to actually find someone I wanted to marry.

He was positive and energetic, open-minded and curious; *and* I found him to be attractive and funny. What more could a girl want? He was right, all the minimum requirements were met, and more. Before we went home, we made plans to see each other later that week.

Suddenly, we were hanging out several nights per week and texting practically every day. After a couple weeks we started having sex and sleepovers. Being with each other filled voids we both felt in our lives at the time, but we also had a lot in common in the way we viewed the world. I felt so connected to York, I even stopped using apps and told Lyle I couldn't see him anymore.

Unfortunately, we were both spending the majority of our time and earnings on intoxicating ourselves so we could forget about how hard we were working to stay afloat. Our collective drinking and smoking problems coupled with my inability to recognize my own issues surrounding sex were a disastrous combination. We were both digging holes.

After a few consecutive days of hardly hearing anything from him a few months later, I became insecure in our relationship. Waiting for his text messages became increasingly painful as it seemed like they were growing further and further apart—I knew what was going to happen next. I began to panic.

My first instinct was to figure out how to keep him from leaving me, a reaction that has never worked in the history of ever. To the internet I went; it was time I consult the "professionals." They would surely know what to do; they could teach me how to navigate these rough waters so I could steer our ship through the storm.

Some of the best and most disastrous advice I've ever applied to my dating life came from the internet and magazines; and advice was consistently unreliable. Remember "dot-dot-dotting" from Xerxes' chapter? I mean, *come on*. I learned there's no "one piece of dating advice fits all," just like there's no diet pill or pair of jeans. Every scenario is different because every relationship is unique; I didn't need to get involved with hundreds of people to figure that out. Relationships are built on trust. No one understands your relationship with another individual better than the two of you do. Others are only able to observe from an outside perspective and listen to whatever details you're willing to share with them, and you only have your side of the story to tell. Whenever there is an issue, we're supposed to talk about it with the other person first. Common sense.

With that said, why was I asking the internet?

Some random article I read convinced me that it was time for me to confront York about the future of "us." Where was this going? We were spending a few days a week with each other and I wanted to know if he ever thought about it, yet the entire foundation of our relationship was built on the fact that neither of us claimed to be seeking anything serious and now my intention shifted because I had feelings for him. The experts instructed me to DTR (Define The Relationship), because then, I would be happy, right? Because he would be on the same page as me? Right?

Wrong. It was time to find out the hard way.

"Where is this going?" (Something Felix once said to me.)

York was undeniably caught off guard when I asked as we sat in my car eating fries from our local fast food spot. There are far better ways to initiate this conversation.

"Uhh... I don't know." He didn't want anything serious, we discussed this on Day 1; and looking back, I wasn't ready for that; I don't even know what I wanted him to say. Neither of us were ready for commitment. He never wanted to hurt me but I put him in a position where I was asking for it because my happiness was dependent on his answer. Due to my past experiences, I thought the reason he was distancing himself from me was because he was into a different girl, but being insecure about myself made it unbearable for him to stay in the first place.

After watching Noah swipe around whilst at my most vulnerable just months prior, I believed I must not be good enough for York, either. My friends told me that I had to move on, so I reluctantly reopened my dating apps and returned to the swiping stage. I wanted to find someone who would help get my mind off York since it was too agonizing to focus on him slipping through my fingers and I was too embarrassed to reach out to Lyle since he initially told me this thing with York was never going to last.

That was when I entered the land of Oz; or rather, when Oz invaded my land. Immediately following that series of unfortunate events, I called York. (Remember, bad decisions are like dominos!) I didn't tell him what happened; he would consider me to be an uncontrollable slut like my mother and Edward both felt the need to express to me once upon a time. York was drunk when I arrived; the stench of liquor on his breath was nauseating with each exhale but I was pretty much on his level to drown out what happened just hours before. Then I had sex with him, too, but I was disconnected. I was raped and in no position to share myself with York, but I did anyway. (I did, however, have the decency to shower in between, but only after smoking half a box of cigarettes.) Two penises in one night was a new low for me.

If I didn't sleep with York after how rocky things were; I feared I would lose him *forever*. After we were done, I asked him something I've never asked anyone—

"Will you hold me?"

He didn't say anything, he just wrapped his arms around me and dozed off. For a moment, I felt safe. I felt loved. I felt like everything was going to be okay. All I wanted in that moment was a shoulder to cry on, someone to hold me and reassure me they were there for me, and there he was. We saw each other one time after that before contact was lost; and that night was one of my worst.

After spending hours hanging out, he hadn't made any sort of move on me and I was feeling insecure about it. Every guy I "dated" tried to have sex with me but this night, York was barely affectionate at all. While we were lying next to each other in bed, I asked, "So, are we going to have sex now, or what?"

He was stunned. I was no longer coming from a place of love and confidence, but rather, from fear and pain. We were hotter than the Mojave Desert but suddenly now colder than the Polar Ice Caps. He drifted away like a glacier to sea and I was too stuck in my head to realize how my decisions created the climate change. It comes of no surprise that this was the last time we saw each other for several years. Every ounce of confidence in my body vanished after I allowed the ghost of Oz to deny me of feeling any sort of pleasure during sex until I crossed paths with Xerxes several years later.

York was not responsible for handling my issues, and I certainly wasn't about to tell him I was raped because that would mean I had to admit I went out with another guy. I was sick to my stomach. I wanted York, but wasn't loyal to him based on my assumption that he moved on. Now he was gone and I was shattered. *Obviously there is something wrong with me*, I thought. I kept beating myself up every time something didn't work out. Why did York withdraw like that after several months?

A friend told me I should just ask him. Completely terrified, I wrote him a text. Why did he go? We were growing so close. Hitting send was uncomfortable, but I wanted to know if there was anything I could do to improve myself so I wouldn't scare off the next guy. Maybe his response would help diagnose my problem and if nothing else, give me a place to start. I am grateful he made me feel like I could trust him to ask in the first place. THAT'S the kind of friendship to look for in other people.

Unfortunately, his response was not helpful for my naïve mind, I interpreted it as his way of being nice; like he didn't want to tell me the *real* reason; which I expected to read along the lines of, "I like you but you have a lot of unaddressed issues." He went with the classic (and always honest), "it's not you, it's me."

I watched his social media blow up for months with photos of himself with other girls while I drowned myself in a pool of my own tears. In the same way I always had a lot of platonic male friends, he had a lot of platonic female ones. Were these girls his friends? Coworkers? Were they *dating*? *Hooking up*? Something in between? Why was I so jealous? I couldn't get over the fact that he was gone *because* I was spending all my free time focusing on what he was doing without me. The more attention you give any matter, the more it will eat at you until it consumes you in your entirety. Why was I concentrating on the **one** reason to be unhappy?

Totally not his fault; misery and depression are mindsets.

I chose it.

Mindsets are like the software of human existence and our bodies are the hardware. Everything we do is simply a program we downloaded, were created with or infected by. *Everything we do is a chosen, instinctual, or learned behavior*. We can program ourselves according to however we choose to function because our mindsets are our choice; but we are only capable of doing so after understanding how it operates and the various programs that exist.

Mindsets can be formed as a result of a sequence of repeated decisions but often, we don't even notice these mindsets are materializing. This is how addictions originate. Regrettably, I was unable to recognize this at that time because I was too busy trying to find out how to replace York's void in my life. There was now a piece missing that I needed to replace when I should instead be figuring out what caused that piece to break in the first place. After Noah and York, then the experience with Oz, I was emotionally dead.

With boundaries and standards, we end up in love; but without them, we end up with STDs or in toxic relationships. I was a magnet for issues because I had so many corrupt files on my drive. I continued running programs that weren't working, which didn't leave me any energy to think about what *was*. My love life went down the rabbit hole after that (Preston, Quentin, Ronnie, Simon, etc.).

I was a regular Alice in Blunderland.

***

York and I reconnected after my graduation.

> *I'm coming back to the city in a couple months,*
> *Let's meet up!*

When I initially saw his message, I was skeptical. This guy was a stranger again. What were his intentions? Why did he want to see me? Last time I was heartbroken. He was returning to town to attend an event, so I said I'd be down to catch up. I wanted to hear about what was going on in his life since a lot can change in a couple years' time; it certainly had in mine.

Video chatting seemed like a viable solution, allowing us to "hang out" like we used to, only now from completely different locations on the map. We reminisced on our past and talked about his reasons for returning to the city; the conversation started to flow into life things and stories and so on. One call turned into another, and another. Not a single dull conversation took place; we struggled to say goodnight every time. Some nights we only hung up when one of our phones died mid-sentence. Had it really been years since we last talked? It felt like we were playing beer pong at that bar a couple weeks ago.

Of course when he visited, I was struck with major anxiety because I'd recently reconnected with William and met Xerxes. He slept in my bed, only, not with me, because I spent the entire night on the floor of my bedroom frantically packing for my trip to Europe as I was leaving first thing in the morning. Even though I wasn't in a labeled relationship, juggling three different ones at the same time felt terrible. Then, I got so hammered in Europe I hooked up with two more people. I was ridiculously out of alignment with myself.

Despite my illogical behavior, our calls continued after York visited. It became our ritual. I started allowing myself to open up to him and share some of the things I never admitted out loud, though I was still holding back so many other things (such as the Oz situation). When people talk about baggage, we think they probably had one or two indecent exes. I crammed so much into my luggage, I had no idea what was even in there. After sorting through it, I now see that in many of my relationships, MY BEHAVIOR WAS TOXIC, not the other way around! How did I allow such a thing to happen?!

The more of my past I divulged to him, the stronger my connection to him felt. In the back of my mind, I feared he might walk away again, but what does that even mean? I told myself I would be a fool to allow him to break my heart twice, so I did what I thought I had to do—I ran first. "I'll come visit you before summer," I said, but I didn't. Instead, I connected with Ulric, then Zachariah.

It was around this time that a huge bomb was dropped on my future. The Chlamydia I was gifted with two years prior apparently also came with something else... HPV, and precancerous cells were forming. Both of these things could potentially eliminate any chance I have to create children of my own one day, as well as at some point develop into cancer. I never received the HPV vaccine in my adolescence because my parents pushed the whole "no sex until marriage" thing, deeming this shot to be unnecessary; and since I never had sex-ed, I had no idea what it was. This diagnosis changed everything in my life because I let it.

The book you are currently reading was inspired by York's continuous attempts to convince me to see a therapist. He knew me way better than I knew myself, and he noticed I was carrying a LOT of baggage on Day 1—years before I started journaling.

There was no way he could comprehend what I was struggling with, but he detected that something was off. I was on a never ending rebound loop because I never slowed down long enough to recover when I was hurting; wouldn't that be a better place to start? He suggested I start journaling if nothing else, but for a long time I was far too stubborn even for that. He convinced me to start writing my feelings down since I was so concerned with what people might think of me for going to therapy. *Journaling felt right.* Words are far more powerful than we realize, and I imagine everyone in my life now wishes I would have just gone to therapy instead of this.

Journaling became a habit about a month after meeting Ulric when I met Zachariah. I had yet to truly understand how much York meant to me, and only then would I finally be able to recognize how much he truly cared about me, too. Although he triggered some intense emotional trauma within me years prior, he now extended a helping hand I didn't even know I needed. Without him, I wouldn't have learned any of the things I am sharing with you; so, in a way, he taught all of us a lot about love, dating, and sex—simply because of his suggestion for me to journal since I was too stubborn to go to therapy.

LESSON #25
Without taking time to pause and reflect,
we are unable to identify and learn from the past.

Everyone has problems. Mine felt miniscule in the grand scheme of things; I mean, I had a conventional nine-to-five day job, a college degree, friends, family, my health (barely) and a roof over my head. So what if I had baggage, doesn't everyone? My problems were primarily emotional, there are people out there who deal with far worse. Just the other day I had a conversation with a stranger who shared his story with me about having a gun pointed in his face by a gang affiliate at the age of seventeen! I simply never thought my basic relationship drama had any place in therapy because I thought it needed to be something as life-threatening as that to warrant it.

I was definitely wrong about that.

Anytime I was sad or discouraged or flushed with negativity, I would drown out those feelings by temporarily masking them with a different one (i.e. alcohol, weed, nicotine, sex, etc.). I knew none of that was solving anything, but it was easier to ignore the problem than try to identify what it was. I was poisoning myself—was that not life-threatening enough?

No one will ever fully understand what another person has been through without going through those same things, and how could they? The closest we can get is to *listen* and *pay attention* to each other. Our words and our actions are an art form and express so much more than we are capable of comprehending.

York always circled back when I said things that didn't make sense or when I avoided answering a question. Inability to take responsibility for our problems is self-sabotage. "I am a victim" was the default program running on my drive. The reason I was so lost in love is because I was running around looking for something that doesn't exist because I didn't understand what I was looking for.

Humans are the smartest living creatures in the universe (as we, the modern human, currently know it). Do you genuinely believe we aren't capable of solving our own problems? It's our own fault most of them exist, but we seldom take responsibility for the actions that brought them upon us. Sometimes, all it takes is a different perspective which is why people pay a therapist for theirs. If there's anything I want you to take away from this book, it is to create a habit of journaling regularly. You will begin to recognize triggers and patterns in your own behavior, and may then work on improving the corresponding areas of your life.

It changed mine forever!

I spent years pretending I was okay, and York saw right through my poker face from the start. He was one of two people that ever asked questions to unlock the deeply buried trauma in my emotional vault so that I could save myself. He forced me to acknowledge my past. I was out of control, metaphorically bleeding on so many others simply due to my own unaddressed wounds.

Addictions are the behavioral patterns that stem from placing metaphorical Band-Aids on these emotional wounds. If you scrape your knee and put on a bandage without cleaning it first, it becomes infected. If still not treated, soon this infection will spread to other areas. All wounds must be given proper care and attention, even if the wounds aren't visible to the naked eye!

York helped me recognize that in order to heal we have to first identify where the wound is. He taught me that closeness has nothing to do with our location on the map. He showed me that sometimes we need to give people another chance, so long as they prove they *want* one. He made me realize that sharing is the exact thing that enables us to feel connected. In all my relationships, I closed off my emotions *because* I never understood them, but sharing them is what enabled me to understand them in the first place. I had it backwards. Connection *begins* when we choose to share.

York inspired me to do more than just journal or open up about my past, he inspired me to just be myself. He inspired me to stop wearing a face full of makeup. Very early on, he inspired and influenced me to start running (for exercise) and start using social media to stay connected with people I don't see on a regular basis.

Opening up was a major step, but I was *still* experiencing my reality through the eyes of a victim. There was still so much inner work for me to do, I hardly even scratched the surface. He was my rock when I had no one else, but he is not a rock, he is a person with feelings. There is no combination of words that can express how grateful I am for him. I'll always love him, and the most important thing is that he is happy.

***

After years apart, we were actually going to see each other again in real life. In typical Laura fashion, I managed to successfully complicate our friendship.

Before I visited him, one of our video chats ended when I made some asinine remark about how neither one of us was ever going to find our "soulmate" as long as we're in each other's lives. What does that even mean? This was a wacky ultimatum I never intended. I told him to ignore the comment, but the mere fact that I said it shows where my head was at. Was I really willing to throw him out the window just to get him to commit to me?

When I finally saw him, I arrived with expectations after promising him I would not. I wasn't myself. I was too closed off emotionally the entire time to have any real conversations.

After I left, I didn't talk to him for months, during which time I spent the majority of my days heavily invested in the editing portion of this book, closing the doors on chapters I had a pattern of leaving open, which ended up being the greater part of the overall therapy—trying to figure out what was going on in my love life so I would be able to move forward and feel confident in a relationship. Why were the guys in Part III + Lyle still reaching out to me? Why was I responding to them if I knew we wanted different things?

I felt like I was in the friend zone with York. Because guys always wanted to have sex with me, I was going on tons of these fantasy "dates" with guys expecting one of them to lead to marriage. I believed it was that I just wasn't finding the right person, but in actuality I was trying to find the right person the wrong way. Why did all these relationships and my beliefs about "dating" revolve around sex?

I pushed York away because I thought I was going to get hurt if I didn't hurt him first. I always wanted a monogamous relationship but did not believe I was capable of one, so anytime things felt like they were right, I sabotaged it, and after doing it for a decade I was an expert.

The last night of that last visit with York was perhaps my greatest outburst sabotage of all—I think I yelled, "I can't do this anymore!" at him while we were watching a TV show, offering no further explanation as to what "this" was. WTF.

Finally, after this disastrous decade, I decided to stop "dating" altogether. I was done. I was exhausted. I was confused. I was on a behavioral loop rendering me incapable of finding what I wanted because I continued to repeat the same abysmal habits without addressing them since I had no idea what, exactly, I was doing wrong that was preventing me from "falling in love."

How can you say you love someone and treat them the way I treated York?

***

Running from problems is my first instinct—always has been.

When I was about five, I placed my baby sister in a little red wagon with some blankets, clothes and snacks and tried running away from home. I knew my parents loved me—I had a roof above my head and food in my belly, but for some reason I was a creature no one knew how to deal with and I was always extremely aware of that.

What was I running from at five years old? Love? Why?!

*

TWENTY-SIX

ZACHARIAH

"Happiness is when what you think, what you say,
and what you do are in harmony."
Mahatma Gandhi

Wow, you made it to the end of the alphabet, can you believe it? Have you learned anything? Do you feel like you wasted a few hours of your time or have your thoughts on dating changed entirely? We've come so far together, and honestly, I don't know how I kept myself together this long. Most people would probably give up on love by now.

For several years, Zachariah and I crossed paths without even realizing it. I had a crush at first sight but was far too intimidated to open my mouth and say "hello." I told myself he was too far out of my league; I never had a chance. Something inside me knew I was going to get hurt if I got involved with him—I idolized him the same way lots of women drool over Chris Hemsworth. If kryptonite could spout legs and arms, he was mine.

Let's finish this whole thing off with a bang, shall we?

***

We ironically connected on a dating site rather than any of the places our paths were already crossing. The first time we spoke was sometime after the incident with Oz—I was pessimistic and in a dark place emotionally. At that time I was in no position to be dating, but this guy I was crushing on agreed to have a drink with me so I was going to show up no matter what.

Drinks did not go well; in fact, it was arguably one of the most boring "dates" I ever went on. I remember thinking we had nothing in common. I couldn't think of anything to say, I lacked the confidence to be myself. I stumbled over my words and I was judging every single one of his.

Needless to say, he was not impressed and I didn't hear from him after that. I had a lot of growing up left to do, so I did what I do best—I kept moving, as did he. We continued coexisting in the same terrarium as fellow ants do going about our daily work. We would give a wave and a smile or a hug if we encountered each other in the real world and went about our day. I convinced myself he was unattainable and now, that we weren't compatible anyways.

My goal at that time was to "find a boyfriend," but what's the point of having a boyfriend? Why was that my end goal? What I really needed to be looking for was a therapist, because technically, I had *dozens* of boy-friends. My actual goal was to find a husband but I never actually believed I was capable of committing to one person forever.

Dating is the trial period to get to know someone to determine if you want to spend "forever" with them. The "boyfriend" or "girlfriend" label exists for the purpose of commitment until we decide someone is, in fact, the one person we want to spend a remainder of this lifetime with. Then, those two people may *choose* to marry each other and those labels change to "husband" or "wife." Labels can be dangerous. They are a breeding ground for comfort and hold different value for different people. For years I've been watching people use these labels and continue to reap the benefits of being single, which is the primary reason I have not had an exclusive "boyfriend" since 2013.

At some point after my graduation Zachariah added me on social media. He was living a life we never talked about on our casual date years before, and I was curious to learn more. Why didn't we have conversations about these things when we first met? Who *was* this guy, *really*?

Shortly after returning from the vacation on which I met Ulric and started journaling because of York, I snapped a photo of the skyline at home with a beautiful, old classic car in the forefront while out during my morning jog and posted it to my social media. The *last* thing I had on my mind was Zachariah, but that morning, I was apparently one of the first things on his...

1 New Message

Alongside an almost identical photo of the shot I posted just moments before, Zachariah added—

I just took the same shot! How have you been?

We shared a few messages until we decided to connect for a drink. What had he been up to? I was curious, but didn't want to go into it with any expectations this time because of how poorly I thought our first encounter went. Were we going to have anything to talk about this time around? He was always doing something, on some adventure to somewhere far, far away from here. Like me, he didn't seem to sit still for long. I was always running from someone, someplace or something. Was he, too?

Drinks at a bar, our original plan, evolved into sharing a bottle of wine next to the firepit in his backyard. *Was this real life? Or was I lost in one of my own fantasies?* We talked for a couple hours before our lips were locked and things escalated pretty quickly from there. I wanted him so bad, but refrained from having sex. He tested my boundaries and tempted me; I almost caved. One of the most difficult things to do is say "no" to something you *really* want. This was exactly what I wanted—*to be wanted by him*, but giving in to temptation yields only a temporary feeling of gratification.

"I don't want the first time we do this to be tonight."

Home I went, thinking I would certainly never hear from him again since I turned him down. I assumed he was only looking to hook up and that was all I could really offer anyway since I had yet to go through any emotional work at that point and I still wanted things to work out with York. At this time I had no intention of writing a book or *anything* about Zachariah at all, for that matter.

Sex may not have happened that night, but it did soon after. He was everything a lover should be and I never wanted to have sex with another new person again. I was hooked from the first time he kissed me. Everything was perfect with one exception—nothing ever followed, which I was so accustomed to, I didn't contest it. After one of the first few times we had sex, I put on my clothes and sprinted out the door in hopes that by leaving, no emotions would materialize. I had nowhere to be except anywhere but there. The total time elapsed between his orgasm and me running on the pavement was probably less than five minutes. I convinced myself I already messed "it" up already by having sex with him, but what was "it?" The fantasy I created in my mind? An expectation? A dream?

For most of my life, I depended on things outside myself for happiness because I never understood the concept of managing my emotions, nor that it was something I was capable of doing. Figuring out how to do so was necessary if I truly wanted to change. I was crying myself to sleep every night because I felt so alone. I wanted to love and be loved, but still had no clue what that meant. How can you see something if you don't even know what it looks like?

Dogs are colorblind. Imagine you threw a blue, a purple, a red, and a green ball for your friend's pet and asked it to bring you back the blue ball. Even if they didn't all look the same through the eyes of the dog, he probably still doesn't understand colors in the English language unless your friend trained it before this experiment, so it would not be capable of knowing which ball you asked for it to return. This is a major reason we fail at things—it is not necessarily that we are incapable, but because we are not prepared. I was not prepared for the type of person Zachariah was.

I started doubling down on my cleaner and healthier lifestyle around this time as I started to train for a full marathon. This also consisted of choosing not to give my attention to things that caused me to feel stressed or anxious. Eliminating negativity improved my life in more ways than I ever imagined, but it would prove to be a much more complicated process than I originally thought.

I was a few months free of my slavery to the tobacco industry, and I attribute this success to Allen Carr's book, *The Easy Way to Stop Smoking*. Smoking did a great deal of irreversible damage to my body and other aspects of my life, but because of my addiction to nicotine, I found Carr's book in the first place. He explains to the smoker how their addiction started, and from there un-brainwashes them. The principles I learned about addictive human behavior from his book apply to countless aspects of life; not just cigarettes. He essentially presents the smoker with a master key that not only unlocks the smoking addiction, but ALL addictions...

***

"Laura!"

Who on Earth would know me here?

I spun around to see Zachariah, of course. My first instinct was—*F****. But why was I surprised? Somehow he was always on the other side of every corner; only this time I couldn't run away because I was in the middle of making a purchase. I wanted to stay and talk to him for hours (and I had the time to—the ultimate paradox), but then my connection to him would deepen and I was terrified of that because I was emotionally invested in York.

The more I got to know him, the more I wanted to be with him, but I didn't know how to do that without the lid popping off my metaphorical bottle of emotions. I wanted to stand there and ask Zachariah about his current projects or what he was up to this weekend, *and* I always had the time to, but every time I saw him, my brain stopped working. Never in my life had someone made me so nervous in their physical presence.

"Let's get together soon!"

"Yeah, totally!" I sprinted out the door. My "catch me if you can" attitude conflicted with everything I wanted.

For the rest of the evening, I couldn't get him out of my head. Or the next morning. He was running through my mind like Forrest Gump—nonstop. It comes of no surprise to me now why I was acting so irrationally—I was addicted to the chemistry I felt with him, and now I was allowing that feeling (the *physical* aspect of the addiction) along with my monogamous relationship intention (the *mental* aspect of my addiction, a.k.a. the mindset) to control me instead of controlling my own thoughts and actions [i.e. a skill I am learning through MEDITATION, and will continue to practice for the rest of my life].

The next day, I sent a message while journaling in the café to invite him to my place for the first time following his numerous requests. It wasn't the finest invitation, but he came (obviously). We both stared up at the ceiling in silence. He rolled his head over and stared into my eyes—

"Wait, so you *like* sex?"

What a strange question, I thought. But it was the *way* he asked it that made me really think about my answer—he said it like he was perplexed I would simply *enjoy* the act of having sex, but I never actually thought about it. Yes, *of course* I like sex. *Duh*. But that got me questioning...

<u>WHY</u> *do I like sex?*

Everyone does, right? Unless they haven't tried it? Humans like sex because it feels good and it's a way to really feel connected with someone else. *Why* did I want to have sex with Zachariah? I felt in my gut that it was a bad idea from Day 1, I know what happens when there is sex without love and no amount of sex will change that, but I thought it could because of how things unfolded with

Lyle. I kept sleeping around and hoping the love would magically show up. Emotionless sex is empty sex, the only reward is a brief climax. Was there a deeper connection here with Zachariah? Interactions with him felt authentic. I couldn't figure out *why* it was so different than it was with others, but now I understand—

For almost half a decade I was only having intoxicated sex.

Only after my fling with Xerxes was the act of sex pleasurable again. It was an intimate experience before it was corrupted. Back with Ben, I could *feel* the love! I used to climax all the time.

Somewhere in between Adrian and Zachariah, sex lost its meaning and became more about the ACT itself than the PERSON I was sharing it with. I was *always* intoxicated; whether that be drunk, high, lusting, or some other form of intoxication. I was mentally somewhere else at all times. Sex became a way for me to *feel* loved when I was lonely to fill a void. How did I pretend like I was okay for as long as I did? I inflicted pain on so many people I care about while I was preventing myself from feeling anything at all. I assumed the only thing anyone wanted from me was sex so I gave them what they wanted to keep them in my life. Sex was the only thing I was focusing on because that's what I was always told men want. That's the narrative I was fed my entire life. My logic seemed foolproof. *Guys only want one thing, SEX, so if they get it from me, they will want me*. Simple. If I had a dollar for every time I heard "men only want sex," I would be able to afford a condo on the beach. This phrase has been on repeat since my childhood.

People think they are being helpful by cautioning women that men only want sex because they are hardwired that way, but that's the most irresponsible advice I've ever heard. Not only is this harmful to women by instilling in us that men *always* have ulterior motives, it is also unhelpful to the mindset of men. Males who believe they are hardwired this way are less inclined to take responsibility for their actions since they're "hardwired" to behave in such a way, so this is somehow became an *acceptable* excuse to justify bad behavior. That is completely bogus and I don't buy it. We're all hardwired to have sex and reproduce. Both men and women have urges and are fully capable of controlling them. This concept needs be discussed in Sexual Education if it isn't already. Women can survive a months without masturbating or we can do it every day. Men can, too. Our sex drive, too, is a mindset. The sexual climate is shifting faster than we know how to evolve with it.

Since I wanted Zachariah so much, I slept with him almost immediately because I wanted him and that's what men want, right? That's how all the other men in this book got entangled with me—they voluntarily walked into my web. I had absolutely no idea what I was doing wrong, I'd practically given up, and consequently this book was conceived. York convinced me I had to acknowledge my past, why it happened, figure out how it was still affecting me, and to move forward accordingly; and now I was finally beginning to read through the raw journal entries I started at the beginning of that year. If I ever wanted to get married, I had to figure out where I kept going wrong. There is no way to kill a demon if you continue running away from it, they are only defeated in face-to-face battle.

Twenty-five and a half of my demons later, here we are.

And no, I'm not talking about the men, I'm referring to the twenty-six demonic beliefs and mindsets I wrestled in the process.

***

Again, Zachariah had not reached out in a while, though I must admit communication is a two-way street and I did not reach out to him either. I assumed he got what he wanted from me and moved along like everyone else. Had he, though?

I still thought about him from time to time.

Someone once said the best way to get over someone is to get under someone else. While this is a terrible idea, I'll admit there is some truth in it. It adds a layer of detachment and acts as a distraction from the person we are trying to forget. It fills a physical void but complicates the emotional situation. I now understood how sex for personal pleasure, to fill a void, is addictive. But if it is sex itself that allows us to feel pleasure, we should be able to have it with anyone and experience those same magical feelings if we want to, right? So long as consent is established, trust is there and we feel attracted to each other?

On my next trip to Europe, I searched for the most attractive fellow I could find—we'll call him Zorba. As soon as we locked eyes, I knew I would be "sleeping" in his bed that night. I wanted to have a one-night stand to prove to myself some sex was, in fact, pointless. It took me almost TEN YEARS of sleeping around to realize that. Sad.

Flirting whilst intoxicated is easy. I threw back a few drinks and started dancing on the stage, gazing in Zorba's direction until we made eye contact a few times. My friend wanted to get some more body paint so I joined her on her trip back to the painter, exactly where Zorba happened to be. After my paint was done, I borrowed the brush and painted the same design on his face before returning to the stage to continue dancing. A few moments later, he came after me, grabbed my wrist and whisked me off to the bar. All men really need is a subtle invitation. It's as simple as eye contact and a smile.

Men are attracted to confident women that know what they want, but don't try too hard because they trust it will come to them. Though it's not easy to put yourself out there, if person is interested, they will respond.

After a couple shots, he asked me to join him under one of the cabanas. Per our conversation, Zorba confirmed that sexual behavior was an addiction and let me know he was in an open relationship. I was attracted to him and my body agreed, but I was unable to climax. Flirting while hammered might be easy, but having an orgasm is complicated. Men are faced with trouble maintaining boners after nights of excessive drinking. Why did I have any desire to have sex with strangers in the first place if I was never climaxing?

Sex with a stranger isn't personal. Why not just masturbate? At least then there's no risk of STDs or the involvement of emotions. Sex loses its meaning when we stop caring who we have it with. Upon the realization that I had a sex addiction, sex with strangers lost a lot of its thrill and to this day I have not had sex with anyone new. Simply acknowledging I had a problem was just the beginning—it took over a year to figure out how it impacted the rest of my life and the people in it, and another year to come to terms with that.

All this time I was trying to separate sex and love, and I had achieved exactly that. I had some platonic male friends and a handful of returning sexual partners. Unless conversations take place about emotions, nothing ever progresses, and I was unable to discuss or interpret my own.

For a long time, I hated when people said this—

When you remove sex from the picture, what's left?

***

Zachariah and I continued crossing paths, saying "hello," and me avoiding him like the plague (a phrase with an entirely new meaning in 2020). The whole point of hooking up with Zorba was to get Zachariah out of my head, which turned out to be a complete failure. One morning at 6am, I received a text:

> *How far do you run in the morning?*

Random, I thought, but my teeth were exposed from cheek to cheek. After a few messages, we were jogging *together* in the misty morning air. This was different. We weren't in a place where we could take our clothes off. When we parted ways, he lifted me up off the ground and kissed me. The feelings I prohibited myself from feeling were exponentially amplified in that moment. I rushed inside to get ready for work. With all the rules I placed on myself I struggled to figure out how to connect. I spent so much time trying to separate the emotional from the physical, I forgot how truly amazing it is when they are experienced together, and he was the first person that made me feel like he didn't need anything from me. It felt so natural. Several days later I got a message and we were back outside with our shoes on the pavement. We had more in common that I initially thought. So much to talk about. He was open with me and I felt I could open up to him as well... until we arrived at the subject of dating.

"How's your dating life?" He asked me.

"I'm not dating," I said, defensively. I vowed to myself after my last outing with William that I was not going to be dating for a while. Then Zachariah asked the BIG question—

"What do you want?"

I was frozen like a deer in headlights. I was short-circuiting.

In what, exactly? Life? Love? Or like, right now? He provided no additional context as to how he intended it. Why was I struggling to answer? This is one of the primary things I was trying to figure out when I started journaling, and I *still* hadn't figured it out; York and a few others asked me before, too, but I never really knew what to say then, either. I never made it past this point.

Falling in love, commitment, starting a family—all of these things scared me to death, and now I didn't even think I was going to be able to have those things because of the decisions I made up to this point. From a young age, I always just knew when I found the guy I would marry one day, we'd figure out the rest together.

In response to the question, I spiraled into a sequence of things I didn't want and other statements flooded with negativity. He repeated my exact words back to me, allowing me to hear what I was saying, and I sounded like a complete disaster. All my interactions thus far with Zachariah were aligned with the preexisting behavioral loop I was stuck in and didn't know how to escape from. I created my own worst nightmare. I entered a state of panic and my body began to physically react as well. I had a full-body rash and my face inflated like a balloon until I looked like a Cabbage Patch doll, literally. This was one of the many anxiety attacks I had while journaling or editing the material you're now reading.

I cried and numbed myself of the excruciating emotional pain I was experiencing with some weed. It wasn't him that I was crying over, it was the realization that I was in my own hell. Everything I wanted was right in front of me but I was holding too much in my hands to carry anything new. The following morning, I woke up to a text from Zachariah stating we should keep things *platonic* and he was right—I was in no place to be involved with anyone.

For months I continued to ponder his question. I want to accomplish so many things in this life; it was hard for me to choose one thing or think clearly enough to just simply say that when he asked. All responses are very telling; deep questions warrant even deeper answers. I had no idea what I wanted because I never really gave the question serious thought, I was always trying to figure out how to give other people what they wanted, oftentimes at my own expense. I was seeking instant gratification instead of what I really wanted in the long run. I was alone as a result of the choices I made. Not only was I chasing an idea that I made up in my head, but anytime I found someone who fit the part I ran away. This was also when I gave York the bizarre soulmate ultimatum. I made a bunch of rules for myself that were serving a version of me I no longer was. I was hanging out in the cemetery of my mind where the ghosts of boyfriend's past continued to haunt me. Why was I treating infant relationships like a continuation of dead ones?

My walls were up and I spent almost a decade building them to be higher than I was. This would surely keep out all the people who might hurt me. I was making decisions based on hypotheticals instead of reality. I may live in La La Land, but there is still a clear difference between what's real and what isn't. Zachariah was the exact type of person I was trying to keep out with the rules and walls; someone who would interrupt my behavioral loop. There was no way I could keep running like this.

Before Zachariah and I ever got sexually involved, he asked—

"Do you trust me?"

Trust him? Like, in bed? Or with my life? My feelings? I hardly even knew the guy at that time. No one asked me that before having sex. <u>NO ONE</u>. (Probably because I was never having *sober* sex, so if there ever was a circumstance this did happen, I do not recall it.) The highway to my emotions was always blocked off and the road had been neglected for so long it wasn't even possible to drive there. There was rocks and debris all over the place and in some places the asphalt was uneven or totally missing.

"I trust you... with my body." I replied.

As we lay among the sheets of his bed, one of his arms underneath my neck, sensual music playing in the background, everything felt so right, yet somehow, so wrong. Why didn't I trust him? He was kind and open and honest with me. He was smart, ambitious, creative, honest, genuine, curious, adventurous, and attractive. He treated me more gently than anyone before him. I was too busy projecting my past traumas on him to try to get to know him. Why was I originally so convinced being with him could only be a fantasy? *It was real!*

That was when everything started to click one piece at a time. Everything that I had been trying to figure out since I lost my virginity, since the end of my last relationship, through the years of ruthless dating. Of course I trusted him—

The person I didn't trust was ME.

I was trapped by this idea that I wasn't good enough for him because I was never good enough for myself; I was always letting myself down. I hated myself for having sex with Zachariah before getting to know him, even though he said it was what he wanted. I continued sabotaging myself because I convinced myself what I wanted did not exist and I thought it was better to cut my losses early and hold on to the temporary high and the illusion of living a fantasy life one day as long as I could. How sad.

I never really knew what "dating" was supposed to be like since most of my friends throughout life were men. Some people called regular hang-outs "dates," others didn't—I stopped clarifying with people after York disappeared the first time and no guy ever cared to ask me. I stopped communicating these things because anytime I did, the response was never positive. I was living a loveless life because I thought a relationship required sex and a label to feel complete. People who walked away recognized my needy behavior as such, which would result in my dependency on them for gratification because I was seeking a monogamous relationship while living a polyamorous lifestyle. I *needed* men like an alcoholic *needs* their alcohol or a smoker *needs* a cigarette.

Ten years of emotions were bottled up, which I ignored and numbed with meaningless sex and substance abuse among other various cries for attention. York was the only person who shook the bottle long enough for the lid to pop off; and only then did things start to change. Writing this forced me to look back to the beginning of my journaled decade of bad decisions to try to make sense out of what the hell happened; where my emotions and triggers were coming from, how to identify them and apply what I learned, how to move forward, and more importantly, how I was going to apologize and clean up the messes I made, and accept that some people cleaned up those messes without me. I hurt some good people in the process of figuring out one simple thing.

LESSON #26
Sex for fun is an addiction.

At the time I started all of this, I was waiting for a promotion that was never coming or for my Prince Charming to come rescue me from the hell I created for myself, whichever came first. I had a completely nonexistent dating life because I was devoted to my job. I wanted to find love, but I repeatedly rejected it. I feared that falling in love with someone would give them power over me.

Unraveling my emotions revealed to me how my past was influencing both the present and future in catastrophic ways. I conquered the art of lying to myself so convincingly, I believed I was happy, when in reality I was living a life of other people's dreams, desires, demands and directions while drugging myself up to deal with the deception. I mastered "fake it 'til you make it" and how to live a lie. I never paused, I never waited, I never looked back, I just kept running, pushing forward and pushing away. By the time Zachariah walked into my life I was covered in scrapes and bruises from head to toe, but I was also really good at applying makeup so no one ever really noticed except York.

How could I ever trust myself again if I continued to make decisions that were inconsistent with what I wanted? I didn't even know what that was anymore. In order to figure out, I had to retrace my steps all the way back to the beginning, back to my roots, to remember why I embarked on this journey for love in the first place. I had to eliminate anything else that caused me stress or unhappiness, and only then would I be able to focus on and have time for the things and people in my life that matter.

I never understood love because I was constantly trying to find it in someone else. Intoxication was the only solution that worked for me because it filled the void of the present moment and enabled me to delay solving my problems. Sex was the culprit of almost all of my dating issues because my own intentions were never pure for having it and my behavior was not in alignment with my monogamous mindset.

Every time something felt right, I sabotaged it because I didn't think I deserved it. Every time something felt wrong, I sabotaged myself by giving all of myself to it. I drank a beer. I took a hit. I smoked a cigarette. I popped a pill. I hooked up with men I had no intention of dating long-term because I just wanted to feel wanted. I gave power to my insecurities and allowed negative self-talk to dominate my consciousness. I blamed my troubles on other people, places, or things. I never forgave myself because I was never sober long enough to figure out where I messed up—acknowledging my own actions had to happen first so I wouldn't do those things again. Why would anyone want to be with me if I didn't have a healthy relationship with myself?

No one can fall in love with you if you do not love yourself; and if they did, they would be falling forever; this is what falling for someone who is emotionally unavailable is like. I ran away from love because if I let it catch me, my whole life would change and I was convinced I was happy being unhappy—that's all I ever knew. Thankfully, we change and grow every single day of our lives. We change with what we let inside our consciousness from the outside world. We may even assist other people in changing if we help them remember how to love themselves which is by showing them how we love ourselves, _the only way_. People only change when they want to change, and they only want to change when they are uncomfortable.

Once I was able to take responsibility for the actions that brought forth the things that happened to me could I forgive myself for my decade of bad decisions and trust myself to make better ones in the future. After forgiveness, trust may be restored. For the first time, I am now able to _choose_ happiness. We all have the ability to choose it upon the realization that we are not emotionally dependent on any one or thing outside our self.

We must know what we want and walk in that direction without hesitation or fear of failure; because failure is inevitable and the sooner we accept that, the more successful we become. Teach yourself to celebrate the fact that you made an attempt rather than focus on the failure itself. In life, we regret the things we don't do most and our faults make us the people we are today. We must go after the things we want courageously and cease to allow the _opinions_ of others to influence our direction. Opinions are merely someone else's perception of your shared reality. When someone shares theirs with you, ask yourself: _Is this person a person I look up to?_ Only allow the opinions of those you respect to influence your decisions or you will get lost in their direction.

We cannot love someone else until we love ourselves; self-love is the entire foundation for loving others. We must be completely emotionally independent for any relationship to work because a relationship is simply a connection between two people. This is the appeal of the open relationship—it is rooted purely in trust, and trust creates space for freedom, love, and vulnerability. I was never open to an open relationship because I had unresolved jealousy issues from my early dating years so I avoided them at all costs.

Zachariah taught me how to set boundaries by setting boundaries with me. No guy ever told me that we should keep things platonic before, I had no idea that was even a thing. Most guys just tried to have sex with me and I was okay with it because I wanted to feel wanted. He taught me how to ask better questions by asking me better questions. He was handing me the tools to fix all my problems by demonstrating behavior I never knew existed. He taught me how to love myself by loving himself, just as the other men in this book did in their own way.

Recovery is not an overnight process, healing takes time. Wanting to be better is a goal that has no end and we can achieve it every day of our lives. This book took years of bad decisions, months of daily journaling, dozens of anxiety attacks and phone calls with loved ones, upwards of 70k words, two years to edit, dozens of therapy sessions, and some serious soul searching along with additional unintended damage and plenty of help from people in my universe.

The reward of staring my past in the face was clarity.

History doesn't repeat itself if we understand it.

*

Self-love is...

- a mindset of internal growth
- being honest and patient with ourselves
- emotional independence from all things outside ourselves
- the realization that the things we think we _need_ are often the source of stress in the first place (we _need_ very little in life)
- hearing the negative thoughts within our minds, acknowledging them, and _choosing_ to let it go
- not beating ourselves up when we mess up—_forgiving_ ourselves
- not comparing ourselves to others (we are all on our own unique journey!)
- learning from our mistakes so we may move forward confidently knowing we will do better next time
- facing our fears and not allowing them to hinder us
- trusting we are going to be okay, _no matter what_
- respecting our bodies because it is the only vessel for our consciousness and without it, we are nothing (this includes natural food, daily exercise, meditation, adequate sleep, regular time in nature, sobriety, etc.)
- making decisions that are in line with what we want and trusting our instincts
- slowing down enough to allow ourselves a chance to breathe
- treating other people how we want to be treated (Golden Rule)
- learning something new about our self and our world every day
- pushing ourselves because it is no one else's responsibility to do that for us (unless we pay them, but first, ask yourself—why do I want to pay someone to do something I am fully capable of doing myself?)
- listening to what our bodies are telling us (only once we acknowledge and understand what is causing our pain can we learn to manage it)

- standing up for ourselves and what we believe in
- respecting our time and boundaries
- saying "no" to things we don't want to do
- spending time with people who uplift us
- expressing ourselves creatively and allowing ourselves to feel emotions
- accepting our flaws
- consciously making an effort to improve ourselves
- expecting nothing

...And more.

It is literally anything and everything that you do that is in line with your purpose in life—things that ultimately result in your health and happiness. Just like any other relationship, SELF-LOVE is the relationship you have with yourself.

Self-love is total alignment.

Self-love is the key required to unlock loving others.

♥

SEX VS. LOVE

"The world is a dangerous place to live; not because of the people who are evil, but because of the people who don't do anything about it."
Albert Einstein

When I was young, I constantly thought about when and where I would meet my "soulmate;" I thought he would walk into my life riding a majestic white horse and we would live happily ever after in a fantasyland. We are told it will happen when it's meant to happen, giving us the illusion that meeting them is completely up to chance and outside our control, like all we can do is wait for them to show up. When we are young, we are naïve.

Beginning from a very young age in western culture, women and men are trained accordingly to abide by society's standards, to follow the leader, to ignore our feelings or emotions, to fit into the molds of those before us; and if not, to doubt ourselves for being different. This mindset alone has the potential to turn lively ladies into weak women and genuine gentlemen into proud pricks.

We are all better than that.

Lust is choosing one's body over one's soul. Most of us do this early in relationships because we are led to believe that is the way things work, but only because we don't understand sex and the power it holds. We do irrational things we wouldn't otherwise do when we want something (or someone) badly enough because we are acting upon feelings that arise from the voids in our lives. These lingering thoughts never exit our brain unless we identify what, exactly, those triggers are. We sometimes let ourselves believe these feelings are completely out of our control; but that is simply untrue. Why do we give our past emotions and feelings so much power over the present? Why are so many of us sleeping with our dreams when we can wake up and have them in reality?

We are always in control *unless* we are sleeping.

Once we accept that there are two types of sex, we are able to make decisions that are better aligned with what we want. Who we have sex with, where and when we do it, and the reason we want it should always be considered as most addictions only influence one person, but by definition, sex requires at least two. For a long time, I considered chemistry, the physical feeling I felt with certain people, to impact my definition of love. While chemistry is rare and the best sex does have an exceptional amount of it, think of it more like the feeling you get from your preferred alcohol, favorite Starbucks drink, or brand of cigarette. The things that we are attracted to are unique to each of us because they bring about a nostalgic feeling.

Have you ever thought about what the simple mindset of being "sexually active" does to the way we date and interact with a person we are interested in having sex with vs. someone we don't? How about the all the ways sex used to get our attention to get us to consume more? How much power do you allow sex to have in your life? Your relationships? Is sex and our misunderstanding of the difference between love and lust preventing us from being truly happy *instead* of bringing us happiness?

If sex feels good, why do women hear the phrase when we are virgins, "The first time always hurts?" Sounds either like the way a first cigarette always makes someone cough or the precursor to some type of trauma. If sex always feels good, why do people feel the need to "fake it?" This is an example of lying to make someone hurry up or feel better about themselves; a people-pleasing tendency. If sex feels good, why wouldn't someone enjoy being raped? I didn't. Shouldn't everyone involved in sex be satisfied?

There are numerous industries that financially benefit from the belief that sex itself is pleasurable including entertainment, travel, wedding, and pharmaceutical—the list goes on. Do you think it is by coincidence these industries are the exact same ones asking for your money? Even politics uses abortion to manipulate people into voting a particular way. They make profits on our decision to carelessly have sex with each other.

We place so much emphasis on physical attraction that we put individuals we find attractive on a pedestal. Focusing on a person that makes us physically *feel* something deep inside us can bring out obsessive behavior and withdrawal symptoms mentioned throughout this book in anyone because CHEMISTRY IS ADDICTIVE.

Let's break it down. There are two types of sex—
- sex from a place of LOVE (choice)
- sex born of LUST (primitive)

There are two different states in which we have sex—
- SOBER (choice)
- INTOXICATED (primitive)

There are two different intentions why we have sex—
- Sex for FUN (choice)
- Sex for PROCREATION (primitive)

Sex for FUN is exactly what it sounds like. This is the drunken one night stand, the casual relationship, the friend-with-benefits, the cheating, the so-bad-its-good, that time on the balcony, the quickie on a lunch break, the "Oops, you were an accident." It happens naturally, but is interfered with by means of a condom or birth control, or is not formal intercourse itself, so that an offspring is not the intended outcome. This is the sex most people are referring to when they talk about wanting sex. This is any variant of sex that is not biologically intended to result in pregnancy (straight sex with protection, LGBTQ sex of any form, oral sex, etc.) The kicker is that no one *needs* these types of sex, *we want to do it* because it's fun and it feels good, and it's a way to connect with a partner. Is it ever fair to demand a partner to satisfy our "needs?" Absolutely not. SEX FOR FUN IS MUTUAL MASTURBATION, you're just using someone else's body parts for personal pleasure. It is an activity two (or more) people do together because they trust each other and they enjoy doing it together. Can you say orgasm?!

Sex for PROCREATION is sex in its most pure form. It is as natural as it is in documentaries about bats, chimpanzees and wolves. Unfortunately, this type of sex is heavily exploited by religion, acknowledging only this one type of sex as acceptable behavior. Religious bodies typically shame those who are promiscuous. Religion has been used to control and regulate the masses since its roots, especially women.

There are two different types of relationships. These two concepts determine our mindset surrounding sex—
- the EXCLUSIVE relationship (monogamy)
- the OPEN relationship (polyamory)

Monogamy is when two people are exclusive with each other sexually and emotionally. When one person wants to have sex and their exclusive partner decides to withhold it (for whatever reason), tension builds. This tension can be released through masturbation or misdirected by cheating, which can range anywhere from consuming porn, having a one night stand, to talking to someone else; whatever you and your partner consider to be such. This is the choice you make when you want to be exclusive.

When a person physically cheats, what happens next depends on the strength of the friendship, which doesn't necessarily mean the relationship ends. In the grand scheme of things, emotional cheating is far worse. An insecure person will experience jealousy if their partner wants to be sexually active with other people which can be a major issue in both exclusive and open relationships. A person who believes sex should be shared with one person can't morally have sex with multiple people.

I spent a decade of my dating life struggling to justify my enjoyment for sex while chasing exclusive relationships with people I wasn't being exclusive with. Even if the other person *wanted* an open relationship I was too scarred from my relationship with Edward to be open to one despite how much it fit my lifestyle—that of a sex addict. Early on, I just wanted to have sex to lose my virginity and eventually, I forgot why I wanted to have it because I never had a meaningful reason to do it to begin with.

What defines the "perfect sex life?" How do you measure that? Is it quantitative? Qualitative? How is it so that two people can have sex and one enjoy it, but the other not? If sex is something you can be "good" at, how would you measure that?

The more confused we are, the less we are able to identify the issue and instead continue along as though there isn't one. It is impossible to solve a problem unless it is acknowledged in the first place. "Good sex" is entirely dependent on the connection between the individuals having it. Without intimacy, sex is empty, and meaningless sex is forgettable. We all want to be loved and trusted and in order to receive those things from others, we must choose to love and trust them first without expecting it in return. The only way we are capable of identifying loving behavior is by loving ourselves unconditionally. Two people fall in love when they love each other the same way.

The domain of monogamy was never intended to be a place where we have sex all the time for fun. This act has been made possible due to advancements in science and technology. Condoms and birth control were invented to enable humans to have sex with more pleasure and fewer long-term consequences. This was great news for our instinctual, physical beings, but catastrophic for our emotional souls as we learn to decipher the influence of CHEMISTRY and the effects of sex addiction on our souls. Sex does not exist to be an activity we do for fun, but as a species, we figured out how to manipulate the act itself so consequences are minimal.

If we didn't have sex for fun, we wouldn't need to spend money on condoms and birth control. We wouldn't need to ride the same emotional roller coasters or sit through rounds of hormonal bumper cars. We wouldn't need to worry about catching STDs. Along with a plethora of others, these are all problems we created for ourselves when we made it acceptable to have sex for fun with anyone so long as it's consensual. The more we want something, the more we are willing to sacrifice for it which becomes very dangerous. When we believe we *need* something, we will stretch ourselves to obtain it, sometimes doing erratic things that fall outside of our personas; things we wouldn't otherwise do.

In my opinion, the *best* sex is SOBER sex for FUN when both LOVE and LUST are present. The best sex has *meaning*. Modern dating culture has completely destroyed the morality of sex in society. Alcohol is perhaps one of the most destructive forces in ALL relationships. We are all more inclined to have sex or try to when under the influence of this substance because it lowers our cognitive function and decision making skills, returning us to more primitive behavior.

Sex is our creator. Does this make it the meaning of life? Without it, we are entering this reality in a loveless lab for someone else's purpose. As science propels us towards a new world where not even sex is our architect and we are merely born when two parent cells find each other in a petri dish, what, then, will sex be? Will it mean anything?

Future generations may only know sex for its exploitability if things continue down the path we are currently on. The primary struggle with our dating culture today is that we are fixated on finding love elsewhere instead of within ourselves. Once we are able to achieve this, we can choose to be with anyone who has reached the same level of self-awareness; any person who is also independent of the outside world for their happiness. We must openly love others without expecting anything in return.

Love is unconditional, which means we must choose to forgive even the darkest things from the past of those we love. Internal peace results when we learn how to coexist with our demons. No one is perfect. Conditional love is fake love, and fake anything is a lie.

Love is truth. Love is forgiving. Love is facing our fears. It is striving to do better and getting out of comfort zones. Love is having difficult conversations and making each other a priority even when it means we have to say "no" to something else we might want. Love is letting go. Love is lifting others up; not tearing them down. It is extending a helping hand, not stepping on someone when they are bleeding on the floor. To unite, not separate. To forgive, not hold grudges. To be present, not living the future or dwelling on the past. To love is to trust, to hate is to fear.

Love will always be a mystery to those not in it.

The only way is to first learn how to love yourself.

There's a lot of stuff out there that will tell you love is hard, people are hard to love, etc.; but taglines like these instill the belief in our minds that working hard for love isn't going to be worth it so we're less inclined to even try, but it *is* worth it. The things we work for are the things we end up valuing most in life. Love is always worth it because it is a choice, and if you aren't satisfied with your choices, you should probably be making different ones. Pain is our greatest teacher and love is our lesson. Anyone who leaves you, treats you differently, or puts you down for not meeting their sexual needs does not love you. Love is the absence of needs.

There is no equation or magic potion that results in love. Love is pure magic, a force unseen by the soul not in it. Love is a deep friendship. Love is light. Love is the only kind of connection worth trying or dying for. Love is a story, not a textbook.

As I learned years ago, love is our choice.

Choose faithfully. Choose wisely. And if you choose correctly, it's a choice you'll only have to make once.

*

THAT WAS THEN, THIS IS NOW...

"Unless you love someone, nothing else makes sense."
E.E. Cummings

Oh yes, I know you've probably been dying to read this part, but I'm here to disappoint you, especially now amid this new bizarre dating world brought forth by this pandemic. If you want to know what my current relationship status is, who or what I want, I can say that I am still single and the rest is none of your business. The events covered throughout this book took place at least a year prior to its completion and since then, I have focused primarily on learning how to love myself. Anyone who stayed in touch with me during this time did so by choice and were made aware I was writing this and not actively dating. Coming to terms with my own addiction issues makes the prospect of dating new people incredibly difficult; who would want to fall in love with someone addicted to sex?

I thought I was destined to be alone for eternity and that I would die in my solitude of old age and be eaten alive by cats so long as my allergy to them didn't kill me first. Though this is undeniably still possible, I will fight for it to not be my story until that day arrives.

I was secretly hoping that after coming this far, I would be in love with one of the guys I wrote about in this book, and the truth is, I was already in love with York but didn't think I was capable of being in a long-distance relationship with him (or anyone, for that matter), my purpose for sabotaging it. I wasn't confident in my own ability to refrain from hooking up with other people because I never understood why I wanted to. Recounting the events that led to the realization that I was using sex to fill voids allowed me to see how much some of the guys in this book actually cared about me. The universe has a weird way of connecting us with the right people at the right time, and we were all in each other's lives for a reason.

***

We cannot go on an adventure for love in our lives with someone else if we expect them to carry our baggage for us; even if they offer. It will only get heavier and at some point they won't be able to help anymore. If we're unable to carry our own baggage, why should someone else be responsible to lug it around for us?

We have to show up to new relationships with an empty suitcase. I was holding on to the fear of being used and manipulated from my relationship with Edward and so many others after him. I was clinging on to the belief I wasn't attractive enough as Noah swiped around for other girls while I was still lying next to him naked in his bed. Apprehension of abandonment lingered in the backpack of my mind from the times York, William, Preston, Caleb and others disappeared without an explanation after months of getting to know each other. The deck of cards sitting in the front pocket of my bag was a reminder that I might eventually grow bored, like I did with Ben and Gaspar. Oz stole my passport so that I got stuck trying to get through security, leaving me stranded in the airport from that day forward. Worst of all, the bag itself was made of the fabric of societal norms and woven together with threads of the generational family trauma passed down to me during the earliest years of my life.

All these added tons of unnecessary weight to my luggage, but the heaviest part was that I was too weak to trust myself to carry it alone. I kept preparing for my trips but sabotaging myself by forgetting to set my alarm the night before and kept missing my flight. I missed my chance with a lot of great guys by holding on to the past.

Why was I still carrying all this around through the airport security checkpoint of my love life? I never unpacked after these "trips," nor did I make a packing list or even check to see what I was already carrying. I never paused to reflect on anything that happened, I just kept re-Tetris-ing the contents of my luggage until all my options were exhausted and the bricks reached the top of the screen. It was impossible for me to get anywhere until I made a conscious decision to clean out my luggage, apologize to myself and people I mistreated, accept things for what they are and promise myself I am going to make better decisions moving forward—but this time, not better bad decisions, just BETTER ones. Everything in my reality is a result of a choice I made; I'm the one who packed my suitcases after all.

When I travel, all I bring with me is a backpack. I don't need much; none of us do. One major thing I live by is this—

Less is more, more is stress.

Simplicity is the ultimate objective.

My entire life I held myself prisoner in a cell of insecurities I built from the bricks of my own labor because that's what I was trained to do. Our walls don't just keep others out, they also isolate us inside. Most people see walls and don't bother, they just take a different path. Some rebellious ones will attempt to climb the wall, research a way around it or bang their head on it a couple times. Only those who *really* want what's on the other side will go to extreme lengths to demolish it completely.

There is no fuel left in my tank to continue chasing the empty highs I once did. It fades to nothing but a lonely hangover; the lingering craving for another sensation just to feel normal again, and in the case of being **INTOXIDATED**, *needing* someone else to have sex with so we can feel loved. We each hold the power within us to love ourselves, we don't NEED anyone or anything. We can CHOOSE to love by expecting nothing in return.

I was always expected to be a successful, independent woman, so I did, but when I got there (as far as what fits society's standards), I discovered there was little that was truly meaningful in my life. Only after driving myself emotionally into the ground and around the country did I learn how to genuinely love, trust, respect myself and be appreciative for all of the wonderful people in my world that make it a better place. Like anything in life, the only way to truly understand something is to experience life both with and without that thing. The void I was trying to fill my entire life was my void of *SELF*-love.

Loving anyone can be hard; but living without loving yourself is even harder—not a single thing on this Earth will make you more miserable. The self-love void is the root of all addiction. It is choosing instant gratification despite knowing it's harmful consequences. Temporary highs leave nothing but a lingering craving for more because gratification provides only an illusion of happiness.

I chose to love so many people who didn't love me in the way I needed or wanted to be loved, I wasn't even able to notice when someone did. We have to learn to love ourselves first. It's like when you're in an airplane and they're telling you what to do when it all goes down, the FIRST thing you're supposed to do is make sure you get yourself hooked up to the oxygen mask before you even begin to focus on getting air to your child sitting next to you. If you can't breathe, you'll die before you help them breathe.

Since I started this process, I spent a great deal of time mourning the loss of the dozens of fantasy relationships I never had—but maybe that's just another place I was wrong... I spent so many years getting to know these guys, I grew to deeply care about all of them but I was never able to focus on one because of my addiction to sex and severe drinking and smoking problems. They all deserve to be treated like kings, and one day they will. A lot of them already are!

This is totally corny, but the process of creating this book gave me something even better than falling in love with someone else; the realization that I have to be in love with myself—because *that's* where it has to start. Once you realize how much of a choice love actually is, you and the person you choose mean that much more to each other because even against all the drama and history, childhood trauma, millions of other people available to swipe, past memories of pain and heartbreak, for some peculiar reason, you choose each other.

For the first time in my life I actually have a healthy relationship with sex and knowledge of what it means to love myself and someone else, so if and whenever we connect, I have a chance at recognizing it next time around.

What we want from a relationship isn't sex, it's intimacy.

A best friend. That's what I want.

♥

*

Connection Timeline

	2007	2008	2009	2010	2011	2012	2013	2014	2015	2016	2017	2018	2019
January		A	B	B	B	E	E	L/N	-	W	-	Y	Y/Z
February		A	B	B	B	E	F	L/V	-	-	L/V	U	Y/Z
March		A	B	B	B	E	-	Y	-	-	-	Z	Y/Z
April		A	B	B	B/C	E	G	Y	-	-	-	Z	Y/Z
May		A	B	B	C/D	E	G	Y	-	-	-	Y	Y
June	A	A	B	B	C	E	G	O	R?	-	Y	Y	-
July	A	B	B	B	E	E	G	-	S?	-	L/X	Z	-
August	A	B	B	B	E	E	H/I	-	W	-	X	W/X	-
September	A	B	B	B	E	E	J/K	Z?	W	-	W	W/Y	-
October	A	B	B	B	E	E	L	P?	W	-	T/Y	Y/Z	-
November	A	B	B	B	E	E	L/M/N	-	W	-	Y	Y	-
December	A	B	B	B	E	E	L	Q	W	-	Y	Y/Z	-

*This is mostly an estimate from 2013 onward.

*

*

To my future husband—

When I wrote this, I didn't know who you were.

Thank you for loving and accepting me as
the master of disaster that I am.

Thank you for allowing me to be myself and for believing I can do
anything I put my mind to. I want you to feel the same. ALWAYS.

If you made it this far and still want me,
I hope you know what you're in for.
It's going to be a wild ride.

...but one thing I know for sure is we wouldn't have it any other way.

♥

*

♥

*